Crushing It with Social Media Marketing

Discover Top Entrepreneur Viral Network and SEO Strategies for YouTube, Instagram, Facebook, Twitter While Advertising Your Personal Brand and Business

Donald Reammsei

Disclaimer Notice

Please note the information contained within this document is for educational and entertainment purposes only. All effort has been executed to present accurate, up to date, and reliable, complete information. No warranties of any kind are declared or implied. Readers acknowledge that the author is not engaging in the rendering of legal, financial, medical or professional advice. The content within this book has been derived from various sources. Please consult a licensed professional before attempting any techniques outlined in this book.

By reading this document, the reader agrees that under no circumstances is the author responsible for any losses, direct or indirect, which are incurred as a result of the use of information contained within this document, including, but not limited to, — errors, omissions, or inaccuracies.

Contents

Chapter 1:
Social Media Marketing Explained in 15 Minutes

Social Media Marketing is a kind of internet marketing that exploits social networking websites as a tool for the promotion of sites. This, in turn, enhances traffic towards them, allowing them to learn from the direct reaction of users.

In recent years, social media has become an essential agent in the growth of businesses worldwide. Yes, social media marketing is gradually becoming a trend among organizations.

Social media marketing, simply defined, has to do with promotional activities which take place through social media channels, like blogs, social media networks and online discussion groups.

Social Media Marketing has to do with the principle of organic search. It means that when a site or its linked social network page has more activity, the position of the website on search engines goes up in their search results, perhaps even making it to the first page.

Seeing as more than 80 percent of users searching the web don't search any further than the first page of search results, and that 70 percent click only on the first three choices, it is apparent that aiming to get on the first page of search results should be your primary goal when optimizing a site.

What Is SMM Used For?

The major objective of Social Media Marketing is to enhance interaction with users, boost the visibility of brands and reach more potential clients.

Social Media Marketing is done by developing quality content which social network users will be able to share with their friends through the transmission of information electronically.

The essence of social media marketing it to obtain feedback from users or possible clients directly so that the company appears more human-like.

By using interactive options on social networks, clients can be heard, either by making complaints or asking questions. This kind of social media marketing is known as Social CRM (customer relationship management) and can result in boosting ROI and credibility. Of course, this is only applicable if users are satisfied with the relationship with the organization, content and the service offered.

Social Networking Sites

Crushing It with Social Media Marketing

Social networking sites allow businesses, individuals and other organizations to communicate with each other and grow communities and relationships online. When organizations become a part of these social platforms, customers will be able to interact with them directly. This level of interaction tends to be more personal to users as opposed to the standard method of advertising and inbound marketing.

The ability of the internet to reach almost anyone across the world has offered the online word of mouth an extensive reach and a powerful voice. The ability to quickly change service or product acquisition, buying patterns and activity to a growing number of customers is said to be an influence network.

Social networking websites and blogs give followers the ability to repost and retweet comments others make in regards a product being promoted, which takes place a lot on social media websites. By posting publicly, friends of these users will also be able to view the message, thus getting across to more individuals. Because product information is being exposed and repeated, it leads to more traffic for the company or product.

Social networking sites are based on developing virtual environments which let customers express their values, wants and needs online. Social media marketing then links these audiences and consumers to organizations that have similar wants, needs, and values.

Using social networking websites, companies can stay in touch with followers individually. This level of personal interaction can inspire a sense of loyalty in followers and possible clients. Additionally, by deciding who to follow on these websites, products can reach a very more targeted audience.

Social networking websites also consist of lots of information regarding what services and products prospective customers may have an interest in. Using new semantic analysis technologies, marketers will have the ability to point out buying signals from questions posted online and content shared by individuals.

A knowledge of how buying signals work can aid sales individuals in targeting prospective clients. In can also aid marketers in running micro-targeted campaigns.

In 2014, more than 70 percent of the business executives singled out social media as a core aspect of their organizations. What is more, business retailers have observed over 100 percent increases in their earnings from social media marketing.

What Are the Most Recognized Platforms of Social Media?

The most popular websites for social networking that businesses can benefit from include:

- Facebook – which has more than 2 billion users

- YouTube – the biggest site for video networking with more than a billion active users monthly

- Instagram – sharing of images with more than 800 million users monthly

- Twitter – broadcasting of messages with more than 300 million active users

- WhatsApp – audio, messaging and video communications with more than one billion users

- LinkedIn – the biggest network of business professionals with more than 400 million members

- Pinterest – Image sharing and collection with more than 150 million active users monthly

- Quora – knowledge and information exchange

- Tumblr – photo sharing and blogging

Benefits of Social Media Marketing to Your Business

Nowadays, almost every individual is on one form of social media or another, irrespective of if this is Twitter, Instagram or Facebook. Social media has become a modern wonder, and instead of being utilized solely for communication which it once was, social media has become a core aspect of any individual who is getting into the world of business.

Now, organizations know how to utilize social media and promote themselves in the best way possible to their potential audience. If you know how to exploit social media, it can become a fantastic tool that will aid in growing your brand.

But, if you still don't see any reason why your business needs a social media page, let us look at some of the reasons why.

Enhanced Brand Awareness

Social media is one of the budget-friendliest methods of digital marketing utilized in syndicating content and enhancing the visibility of your brand. Executing a strategy on social media will significantly improve the recognition of your brand because you will be engaging with a broad consumer audience.

To begin, develop social media profiles for your organization and start to interact with others. Get business partners, employees as well as sponsors to share and like your page. Just by having individuals interact with your content, your brand awareness will go up and start to grow your business reputation.

A new network of individuals is likely to see each shared post. This can result in them becoming potential clients. What is more, the more individuals who know about your organization and what you do, the better. By investing just a few hours weekly, more than 90 percent of marketers claim that their efforts on social marketing tremendously enhanced their exposure.

Without a doubt, just having a social media page for your brand will be beneficial to your business. Also, with frequent use, it can produce a broad audience for your business

Increase in Inbound Traffic

If you do not market your organization on social media, your inbound traffic will be restricted to your regular clients. The individuals who know your brand are possibly looking for similar keywords you rank for already. If you do not use social media as an aspect of your marketing strategy you will find it more difficult to reach individuals who are not in the circle of your loyal customers.

Each social media profile you include to your marketing mix opens a path to your website, and each content piece you post is another chance of getting a new client. Social media is a place filled with various kinds of individuals who come from diverse backgrounds with varying behaviors.

With different individuals come varying needs and diverse methods of thinking. Placing your content on as many platforms as you can lets these individuals reach your business organically. Perhaps a person in an older consumer demographic will look for your site using a specific keyword on Facebook, but a younger client may start their search by utilizing another platform of social media entirely because they don't search for products the same way.

When you market on social media, you can open your business to a broader range of varying customers around the globe.

Enhanced Rankings on Search Engines

When you post on social media, it may help your business gain some traffic. But if you want a significant level of success, you would have to put in more effort than that. Search engine optimization is crucial for attaining higher rankings on your page and drawing traffic to the site of your business.

Although social media does not increase search engine rankings directly, it was stated by Social Media Examiner that over 50 percent of marketers who have been utilizing social media for a year or more would see better search engine rankings. The ability to rank lead positions for keywords will transform your traffic and keep producing positive results for your organization.

Speaking factually, almost everyone utilizes Google in finding information, and there is less likelihood of them navigating further than the first page because they usually find the solution to their queries there.

If the website of your organization does not have a high ranking on search engine results, you may likely have to make changes to your

SEO strategy, so that you have the best possibility of getting a better ranking via social media. To do this, you need to produce content of high-quality that incorporates your target keywords.

Content like case studies, infographics, employee photos, and business information wi l make the social media profile of your business credible and exciting. The instant you start posting content of high-quality, you will begin to grow a social media environment where followers will share and like your content.

The important part is, it gives you the chance to get in front of industry influencers who will write about your organization and offer linkbacks which will aid directly in enhancing rankings on search engines.

Higher Rate of Conversion

When your business has more visibility, it will have more chances for conversion. Every video, image, comment or blog post may direct viewers to the website of your organization and enhance traffic. Social media marketing lets your business offer a positive impression by utilizing a humanization factor.

When a brand is interactive by commenting, sharing content and posting statuses on social media, it helps personalize it. Individuals would instead do business with other individuals as opposed to companies. Over 50 percent of marketers made claims that taking the effort to groom relationships with customers proved positive results in sales.

The better your impression on a visitor, the higher the probability of them thinking about your organization when the need for your services or products arises. According to studies, social media has a 100 percent higher lead-close rate as opposed to outbound marketing. When a brand has more interaction online, customers who follow the accounts of your brand often start to trust your business's credibility more. People generally utilize social media platforms to remain connected to their family, friends, and communities. Since individuals are interacting already, why not add your brand to the conversation? Most times, they will tell a friend about your brand when your services and products are required.

Placing your brand in an environment where individuals are talking, liking and sharing can only enhance the rate of conversion on your present traffic.

Enhanced Customer Satisfaction

Social media is a platform for communication and networking. It is crucial to create a voice for your company via this platform if you want to humanize your organization.

Customers love knowing that any comments they post on your page will get a personalized response as opposed to an automated message. The ability to acknowledge every comment show that you listen to the needs of your visitors and have the goal of providing them with a peak experience.

Each customer interaction on the social media account of your organization is a chance to publicly show how compassionate you are to your customers. Whether a person has a complaint or question, social media lets you dea with the matter utilizing interpersonal conversation. A brand dedicated to the satisfaction of customers, which takes time to write a personal message, will be seen in a positive light, even if responding to the complaints of a customer.

Enhanced Brand Loyalty

One of the core objectives of almost all organizations is creating a loyal customer base. Considering that brand loyalty and customer satisfaction go alongside one another, it is crucial to engage customers regularly and start creating a bond with them.

Social media is not just restricted to introducing the promotional campaigns and products of your brand. Customers view these platforms as a channel where they will be able to communicate with the business directly.

The millennial generation has the most brand loyal customers. They make up a more substantial portion of the US and will soon take over the market entirely. According to studies, this group of customers is more than 60 percent loyal to brands that interact with them directly on social media.

Since this group needs communication with their brands, it is essential that organizations implement social media marketing to draw their attention as they are the consumers with the most influence.

Increased Brand Authority

Brand loyalty and customer satisfaction have a role to play in ensuring your business is more authoritative, but it all boils down to communication. When consumers observe that your organization posts on social media, especially posting authentic content and replying to customers, it makes you seem more credible.

Frequently communicating with customers shows that your organization cares about the satisfaction of clients and is available to provide answers to any queries they may have. Happy customers are elated to spread the word about a fantastic service or product, and social media is the location they usually head to to express their thoughts.

When customers mention your organization on social media, it will aid in advertising your organization and show new visitors your brand's authority and value. As soon as you can get some satisfied clients who are happy to talk about their excellent buying experience, you can sit back and watch real customers who benefited from your service or product do the advertising.

Cost-Efficient

Social media marketing is perhaps the most cost-effective aspect of an advertising strategy. t is free to sign up and create a profile for almost all platforms for social networking. Also, any paid promotion you decide to invest in does not cost that much in comparison to other marketing strategies.

Being cost-efficient is such a great benefit because you experience more ROI and invest a larger budget for other business and marketing expenses. If you choose to go with paid advertising on social media, it is crucial you begin small to see what is to be expected. As you become relaxed, make changes to your strategy and try adding more to the budget. Ey spending a little amount of money and time, you can drastically enhance your rates of conversion and get a return on your initial investment.

Attain Insights to The Marketplace

One of the most significant benefits of social media is marketplace insight. There are no better methods of knowing what your customers need and think than by speaking to them directly. By observing your profile's activities, you w ll be able to see the opinions and interests of customers that you would not have previously been aware of if your business had no presence on social media.

Using social media as a support tool for research can aid in gaining valuable data that will help you better understand the industry, once you have amassed a considerable following, you will be able to use additional tools to investigate your consumers demographic.

Another aspect of social media marketing, which is quite insightful, is the ability to section your content syndication lists based on topic and point out the kinds of content that amass the most impressions. With these tools, you will have the ability to measure conversions using posts on a variety of social media platforms to find the ideal mix to increase earnings.

Thought Leadership

Posting properly written and insightful content on your social media page is a fantastic method of becoming a leader and expert in your industry. Becoming a leader requires work, and you can get assistance by using online tools. To become an expert, you need to make use of social media channels and develop your presence.

Be interactive, share content, bond with your audience and promote your authority. When your social media campaign aligns with your other marketing efforts, it will highlight your skills and your audience will look up to you. The ability to connect with your customers directly results in a relationship that they will find valuable. This lets you become a recognized influencer in your sector.

Chapter 2:
Double Down on Social Media Marketing NOW

Lots of businesses are cautious about the kind of marketing strategies they spend on. When your marketing budget is limited, it is crucial that you wisely spend it to get the best from your investment. Social media marketing is one of the most cost-effective and versatile strategies that businesses can utilize in reaching their target audience and enhance sales over time. This is the reason more than 90 percent of marketers are utilizing social media to get to their audiences.

So why do businesses need to double down on social media now? Below are a few reasons why it is compulsory for small businesses.

You Will Find Your Customers on Social Media

One of the primary reasons why your business must be marketed via social media is because your clients spend lots of time on these platforms. The number of individuals using social media is on the rise, and with lots of customers utilizing social media daily, this offers an excellent chance for businesses who want to reach their audience online.

It can be easy to connect with your target audience if you are active on the platforms that they utilize most frequently. Go to your audience as opposed to waiting for them to come to you. If you are not on social media already, you are probably missing out on a crucial opportunity to interact with new leads and connect with your clients.

Clients Are More Receptive on Social Media

Individuals who are active on social media channels do so because these platforms provide an easy and entertaining method of networking, keeping in touch with family and friends, and keeping abreast of things going on around the globe. Users don't join these channels to get marketed to, but it does not imply that users of social media don't follow and interact with the brands they love.

When users engage and follow brands, it is because they see the information and content in these social media campaigns relevant. Whether these users are enjoying entertaining content, in search of deals or just want to find out more regarding the brands, social media users are more likely to engage with brands through their social media channels.

Clients tend to be more receptive to the message of your brand on social media because social media lets you show another aspect of it. The content you release on these channels contributes to the personality of your brand and aids in demonstrating your brand's voice.

Via social media, you will have the ability to make a real connection with your customers and leads, as opposed to just sending direct marketing messages. Clients are more responsive to this sort of thing.

Advertising on Social Media Lets You Target and Retarget Perfect Customers

Although social media marketing does not need any investment in advance, social ads can do much to support your existing organic campaigns on your social media channels. Using refined targeting capabilities, social media channels like Facebook aids you in targeting your perfect buyers, which lets you push more significant traffic to your website. This is the ideal method of getting the best from your marketing investment.

Through Facebook ads, you can point out new possible leads by defining your perfect customers using the ads platform. Also, Facebook lets you serve your ad content to individuals who show the same kinds of attitude your target audience does. As you push more significant traffic to the website of your brand, you will be able to enhance the results, irrespective of what your ad objectives are.

You Will Find Your Competition on Social Media

Irrespective of the sector you are in or your target market, there is a huge possibility that your competitors are there already and taking advantage of social media platforms. This not only shows that there is a chance for your brand to equally perform well on these platforms, but it also implies that some of your potential clients may be speaking to the competition already.

If you need to stay competitive in the online marketplace, it is crucial that you begin working towards the establishment of a social media presence. Social media content not only gives you the chance to show a little part of your brand's personality, but it also offers an excellent channel for showing your industry knowledge and expertise. This is one of the best methods of making yourself stand out from the competition and bringing in more significant online traffic.

Social Media Marketing Results in Higher Rates of Conversion

Social media has a 100 percent higher close rate than outbound marketing strategies. This could be because every piece of content you upload and interaction you may have on your social media platforms is a chance to transform an attracted lead into a satisfied customer.

By developing rapport with your customers and leads, and posting relevant content consistently, your brand will be able to work at improving credibility and trust, which results in more conversions.

The most important aspect of social media that leads to more conversions is the ability to add a more human element to your brand's messaging. Because social media is a location for customers to network and socialize, brands can show their human side through conversation and simple content that shows their warmth, humor, and personality.

Customers Are in Search of Recommendations on Social Media

WOM (word of mouth) marketing is one of the most reliable tools that any organization has in its marketing arsenal. Aside from the fact that it is free, it goes further in aiding you to develop credibility with new leads. In lots of ways, social media has transformed into a new environment for word-of-mouth marketing. Now, brands are starting to encourage their clients to leave reviews on their social media pages, offer testimonials or recommend their brand to family and friends on social media.

Consumers have a higher possibility of purchasing from brands that others recommend. These recommendations don't have to be from a family member, friend, or co-worker. Consumers have as much a likelihood of trusting online reviews as they would personal recommendations.

Customers are always searching for recommendations on social media, and these recommendations affect their buying behavior. This is why it is crucial that you continue encouraging your satisfied customers to leave a review for your brand on social media and recommend your services and products to others. This is a fantastic method of generating some of that significant word of mouth benefit that aids in increasing sales.

Social Media Can Help Link Your Brand to Clients You Never Knew Existed

Lots of brands depend on PPC ad traffic and search engine optimization to locate and engage new leads. But, marketing via social media can be a fantastic channel for drawing in new clients. Reviews or recommendations on social media can go far in aiding your brand link with customers whom you never knew existed.

Your company can also utilize social media to tap into new markets through other ways. One method of locating new market opportunities and customers on your social platforms is via social listening. By following specific keywords and searching trending subjects in your sector, you will be able to see who is partaking in the conversation. This can aid in providing your organization with loads of chances for new leads while equally connecting you to influencers in the industry which you may be able to collaborate with to enhance visibility.

Top Social Media Marketing Strategies
The factors that constitute efficient social media marketing differ. They depend on a range of factors which include current trends, and your goals alongside your audience. These factors define what your plan of action or strategy to achieve a specific goal should be.

Below are a few of the tried and tested strategies that are almost certain to work alongside other upcoming strategies that can help you keep up with the changing trends.

Developing Different Kinds of Content

It is quite easy to get sucked into only posting brief tweets on Twitter or pictures on Facebook. However, on most social media channels, you can post diverse kinds of content which include infographics, blog posts, and videos. So why do you need to do this?

For one, creating the same form of content without end can bore your audience which will prevent you from attaining your goals. You are going to get the same results you have already if you create the kind of content that echoes with just a part of your audience or worse still, none.

By ensuring your posts vary, you will be able to determine the top kinds of content for your target audience and easily appeal to all its subsets.

Offer Education

Irrespective of the goals you have, offering education is almost the best means of helping you attain them. If you provide relevant information or great advice, individuals will see you as an authority and will likely become loyal clients with time.

You can educate your followers on social media itself or by utilizing your accounts to lead engaged followers to educational resources like webinars, online courses, white papers among others.

Do Less Promotion and More Storytelling?

Going the educational route implies that you will be teaching more as opposed to selling. Storytelling is along the same lines and can be educational. But the strength of storytelling is not in teaching individuals' things they were not aware of but informing them about situations or characters that they can relate with and draw out emotional responses. These kinds of reactions trigger action, usually more effective than continuous and annoying self-promotion on social media.

Use Influencer Marketing

Collaborating with well-connected and renowned influencers is an excellent choice for numerous reasons. Two major advantages are:

It enhances your credibility and provides you access to a broader audience, both of which can aid in making your strategy for social media marketing more efficient.

Take Advantage of The Eagerness of Loyal Clients

Your loyal customers have lots of power. They also can become advocates for your brand. They can enhance your brand awareness and offer great social proof, aiding other customers in developing trust in your organization faster than they would have initially.

Social media is a great tool when used by motivated brand advocates. However, you must be the one to motivate them. You can do this by:

- Requesting reviews on social networks like Instagram and Facebook

- Ensuring the submission of great content generated by users, which can then be utilized in your social media campaigns

- Granting interviews to satisfied clients and publishing their stories to your pages on social media

- Setting up contests and providing rewards, which would then inspire individuals to spread the word regarding your organization on the social media platforms you decide.

These are just a few of the choices you must take advantage of.

Best Upcoming Social Media Marketing Strategies

Yes, lots of strategies that have worked in the past can still work now. However, you need to understand that as technology and trends go through change, you need to implement new strategies. So, what are the strategies for social media marketing you need to take advantage of? Below are a few of them:

Augmented and Virtual Reality

The interest consumers are starting to have in immersive experiences is beginning to rise. Due to this, both AR, augmented reality, and VR, virtual reality, are beginning to be used more as tools for marketing. This could either be via absolute immersion experiences that take you to a world of your own (VR) or via digital factors including a live view (AR). Numerous brands are enhancing audience engagement in this way.

Taking advantage of mobile cameras in this method can give your potential clients the chance to experience and understand your services and products in the same way they would in real life. You would be able to have a direct influence on their purchasing choices, which would have obvious advantages to your organization.

If you have not done so yet, you need to think of ways to include VR/AR into your strategy for social media to achieve your goals in the coming years.

Live Streaming

Live streaming has existed for some time now, but it is still something that needs more emphasis. This is because more than 70 percent of brand audiences would rather choose live video instead of social posts and blog posts.

Generally, as videos keep rising in popularity, you can be confident that there will only be an increase in this presence. Now is the best time to place more focus on streaming and learn to master it

Social TV & Vertical Videos

Lots of social channels are now focusing on vertical videos because people use their phones vertically most of the times. This recent focus goes alongside something else that is gaining popularity known as social TV.

Leading this trend presently is Instagram with the newly released IGTV. It lets users develop channels and upload long videos there. Snap originals and YouTube TV are also similar kinds of social TV, although not presently available to the multitudes.

Still, long-form and vertical videos are things you should consider creating, especially if you promote your business using Instagram and want to try out IGTV.

Enhanced Humanization

Individuals tend to have a strong response to others. If you humanize your brand on social media, you will be able to create a more effective marketing strategy. How do you do this? Well, you need to communicate with your followers as much as you can by using content generated by users, responding to comments, etc. Although these things have already been recommended, it is now more critical than ever.

Chatbots

Chatbots will undoubtedly become more popular on social media in the future. You can use these bots to respond to questions, urge unlikely sales, begin conversations and offer individualized customer support and service.

By incorporating this social media strategy when only a few individuals are utilizing it, you can drastically enhance your results and appeal on social media.

Stories Will Grow More Popular

Stories are now on the rise. Viewing visual content in a vertical layout which lasts for just 24 hours started making waves on Snapchat and soon Instagram followed suit which made it a world trend for individuals of all ages.

Snapchat may have battled since then to stay relevant since that is what it is known for, but now, stories are now on Facebook, Instagram, YouTube and LinkedIn.

Presently, there are over 300 million individuals benefiting from Instagram stories daily, while Facebook is making efforts to incorporate stories in our daily life.

Advertisers have also observed that Instagram Stories ads can be quite efficient, with Facebook and Snapchat keeping up with their present demand hype. So why are stories so great?

- They are not difficult to make

- They depend on authenticity

- They are entertaining

- They don't need more editing before you upload

- They don't last past 24 hours

Messaging Will Rise Even More

In usage, messaging apps have already surpassed social media applications in terms of usage, and it looks like a trend that will dominate the future. People are going past social media posts to private messaging. This is the case simply if it has to do with reaching their loved ones or keeping up with their best celebrities.

What makes messaging appealing is the fact that brands can locate the engagement they desire by understanding how individuals utilize messaging applications.

Earlier in 2017, marketers were of the belief that messaging is the pioneer trend that will have an impact on their social strategies. Messaging, Viber, WhatsApp and WeChat have a huge part of the messaging market and they already unleashed extra features to go past messaging, from news updates and stories to utilizing automated bots for e-commerce and customer service roles.

There is an entire world for brands to take advantage of and lots of huge publishers and brands are starting to exploit the messaging trend.

Chapter 3:
How to Start Social Media Marketing with No Experi-
ence

While making attempts at growing your business, you have concluded that having a strong presence on social media is how to make this happen. Now, a question arises. How do you set about it?

Making your first move on a social media platform is not the easiest of things. There are lots of platforms, as well as sites. These are in addition to the huge number of social media users, and an overwhelming amount of content to check out.

With this, how exactly do you get started? Do you have an exact reason for promoting your business?

It is quite a lot to think about. Below are tips to help beginners with social media marketing.

Set Out with A Primary Objective
There are some critical questions that you must provide answers to if you want to take advantage of social media. What do you plan to achieve? Do you plan to up customer service, or make better sales?

Are you also considering the option of getting your brand into the minds of people?

If you can provide answers to these questions, then, your efforts on social media will be in a guided direction. As the months and years go by, you will have to put more time into social media. As a result of this, you should start with your fundamental objective. This will help you measure the progress you make.

Take One Step At A Time And Be Choosy

There are a lot of social media platforms. Popular among them are LinkedIn, Facebook, Instagram, Twitter, etc. If you have big dreams, there is a likelihood you will want to take advantage of the most famous social media platforms. Well, the truth remains it will be impossible to do so. Don't try to have a presence on all social media platforms all at once. You must take things slowly.

Be careful how you choose. Start with a couple of sites first. These should be the most ideal for the kind of business you do. As soon as you can put in more time, as well as money, get on other platforms and make your business known.

It Is Not Enough to Be on A Platform

It is vital that you have an audience in mind. As you come up with strategies, the question "Who is your audience?" will be a great guide.

This question will influence how you strategize. Think about your choice of site for a second. If your target audience are millennials, platforms such as Instagram, Snapchat, and YouTube will be ideal. Pinterest is surprisingly good if moms are your target. With Facebook, you can reach virtually everyone.

What social platform will be ideal? Well, the answer to this question is dependent on the business you at running. Carry out intensive research on your target audience before making important decisions such as where to put your efforts.

You Should Have A Catchy Handle

If a handle is memorable and catchy, it will stick in the minds of people. As far as your presence on social media is concerned, you should have a handle that can be easily attributed to your brand irrespective of what platform it is on.

You could decide to make use of the name of your company. You could also use something that brings attention to the unique quality that your brand possesses. An example of this is that the BBC makes use of @BBCBreaking as its account name on Twitter. This brings breaking news to the minds of people. Also, Samsung makes use of @Samsung-Mobile. This reminds consumers about the existence of their mobile devices.

What Is the Ideal Handle for Your Business?

As soon as you have decided on the handle to use, carry out adequate research to make sure that it has not been taken on the social media platforms you are getting on. You can get this done using Knowem.

Get A Social Media Team

When you come up with a plan for going into social media marketing, you must create a social media team. You will also need funds to make this a reality. After your presence on social media becomes prominent, handling it all by yourself will be very difficult. You will need to work with people and focus on the actual running of your business.

Make attempts at building a team of professionals with very different qualities. This team should have a writer that can create social content which is compelling, and a video and graphics group that can handle multimedia. That is not all. An expert at analytics will also be needed on your team. This expert will take note of your progress, as well as the weaknesses he sees in your social media campaign. A lot of small businesses do not have the resources to pay individuals for these positions. Well, if you own a small business, you can work with freelancers that are willing to work passionately at lower prices. You can find these freelancers on Upwork or Freelancer.com.

Get the Pacing Right

While making efforts to be active on social media, there are specific questions you need to provide answers to. How frequently will you put up posts on social media? Will you post once a week, or will it be more frequent?

Well, the answer to this question is dependent on the site involved. One basic rule is if you are putting up blog posts that are long, then, it is okay if you make posts weekly or twice a week. If you are posting on such sites as Instagram, LinkedIn, and Facebook, you might have to make up to five posts weekly. This is because people on these sites are used to getting regular content from various brands. You can even make more posts on Twitter. It is okay to have lots of tweets in one day. While at this, it is important to have one thing in mind. Don't just make posts for the sake of posting. Every post that you make must have some form of relevance to your target audience.

Have A Schedule, But Add Some Flexibility

As soon as you can conclude about how frequently to make posts, you must provide an answer to the question "when."

As far as posts on social media are concerned, science, as well as art, is involved. There are certain times which are regarded as perfect for posting because they are periods when people visit social media the most. Normally, people spend time on social media after work and during lunch breaks. Nonetheless, if you make posts only around these times, you will start appearing a little too robotic. This is certainly not what you want.

There are lots of tools for good content management. However, one of the best is Co-Schedule. Co-Schedule is a great WordPress plugin.

Be Authentic and Personal

Getting acquainted with people on social media can be likened to doing so in a social gathering. Just like you need to be yourself and be authentic to make friends at social gatherings, you do not have to pretend to be someone you're not on Twitter.

Always remember this while you make posts online. A lot of people might not be very comfortable getting close to a brand with a social media presence that is not flexible or that is a little too serious. You should have a personality on social media, be warm and interactive. If people find you nice and interactive, you can be certain that they will follow you.

You Should Have A Content Pipeline

A post that is funny can attract a viewer for a couple of minutes. However, if you want to ensure that your viewers keep returning to your page, you must post content that is engaging. If you can get this done, you can be sure that people will come visiting your page.

Ensure that a pipeline for your content is developed. What are the types of content you post? Where and when will they get published? You should have a plan and follow it strictly. However, if your plan is not working well, it is okay to make changes.

Mix Up Your Content Offerings

You cannot share content without having a plan. But really, what kind of content will you share? Well, to do things the right way, you should have various kinds of content. You should be able to strike a balance between your content and content curated from sites that are not yours. You should get content that will be valued by your audience but may be difficult for them to find themselves.

The content which you curate should bring a balance to those you create initially. If the content you share is only from others, it will appear that you are a parasite that takes advantage of the hard work done by others. On the other hand, if you release only content that you create yourself, you might appear like all you care about is promoting your brand. With the right balance, you can seem humble and knowledgeable.

Link, Link, And Link

Again, as soon as the social media presence of your business becomes strong, the next thing to do is get people connected to it repeatedly. You should not make this look forceful so that no one suspects cases of spamming. However, you should emphasize your brand.

The fantastic thing that businesses with more than one social media accounts enjoy is these accounts can all be linked. You can connect your twitter page to a post you put up on your blog. You can put up a photo on Instagram and tell your audience to learn more about it on your Facebook page.

Coordinate from A Central Dashboard

Having multiple accounts is excellent. There is, however, a downside. It can be quite confusing. You have decided to make a post on a particular social media account, but you are not sure which one anymore.

You may need to make use of a tool to ensure that your social media activities stay coordinated. Examples of tools that can be used to coordinate your social media activities are Sprout Social, Hootsuite, and Sensible. With any of these devices, you can have a dashboard that is centralized. Once you do this, you can view everything that is happening all over your social media platforms on a single screen. There are lots of social media management platforms. All you need to do is carry out your research and make a choice of the best one for you.

Add Value for Customers

There is an important question that is usually asked by business owners regarding making posts on social media. That question is "Once I begin interacting with customers, what approach should I take?"

The gimmick is to draw a line between getting personal with your audience and passing the message of your brand across. The aim is to have increased sales without appearing like all you want to do is market. With social media, making people aware of your brand and bringing about increased visibility at the sales funnel's top. It, however, isn't the right place to drive price points.

Your focus should be on increasing your customers' value in ways which are subtle. Give them vital tips. Provide answers to their questions and solutions to their problems. You can go as far as providing strategies which will help them do better in business. You will make more sales as soon as you begin adding value to their lives.

Make Important Business Contacts

Social media is also known as social networking. It is not known as social networking for nothing. There is a reason behind this. This reason is that the internet is the best place to make vital connections. It is important to make use of your social presence in building relationships which will be of help soon.

You can have more than one strategy to make this a reality. With LinkedIn, you can get in touch with people that could hire you in the future. LinkedIn can also help you avoid the embarrassment of gatekeepers at firms you intend doing business with. On Twitter, you can share thoughts with thought leaders of various industries. Bonding with the general public is possible on Facebook. There are lots of opportunities on social media. Take advantage of them.

Don't Be Scared of Trying New Things

For some time now, social media has passed as a productive marketing plan. We have discovered that there are special ways of doing things on social media. There are certain norms that should be adhered to. They include how frequently to post, when, and where to post.

You might follow these rules like your life depends on them initially. That is because doing so will be best for you until you have a good understanding of how things really work on social media. As soon as you understand things better, you can come up with new strategies.

Alternate the timing as well as the volume of content that you post. Put up different posts. Go into fresh social sites that are not so popular. Play around with convention. This might help you discover fresh strategies that will work well for your business.

Track Your Company's Reputation

Social media sites are ideal for putting up details concerning your business. There is, however, a secret - other people talk about your brand. This is not limited to you.

While you browse through different social sites, spend time getting to know your business's reputation. Get to discover what is being said about your brand. If you come across positive comments, show some gratitude for the good comments and promise to continue the right path. If you notice negative comments, try to fix that aspect of your brand.

Measure the Results of Social Media

Earlier in this book, we spoke about how important it is to have a goal when starting. Always have the reason you joined social media in your mind - it could be to have improved exposure or to have better sales, whatever your reason, goals are important.

As you go on, it is important that you keep setting goals to check out how much progress you have made. If an increase in sales was your goal, go through the figures. Have they increased? If better service was your target, try to find out, have you been able to make any noticeable change with your efforts on social media?

Social media is time-consuming. It also requires money and energy. You definitely do not want to skimp on any of these. Making it a habit to constantly check your results will ensure that your efforts are not in vain.

There are lots of social media sites which have several different uses. This is how to get the best out of them.

Start out with primary goals. Think about them when you come up with strategies, an identity, and your audience

Set up your presence on social media with a good volume of content. This content should come from your business, as well as other sources.

Discover new ground, experiment, and follow your success closely. With social media, your business can thrive and grow. Always remember that it will take some time.

Best Social Media Marketing/Management Tools

Social media can be frustrating if you don't have the appropriate tools or knowledge. Irrespectve of what your aim is, you will need the appropriate social media marketing tools.

Below are a few that can make your social media process as seamless as possible.

Buffer

This is one of the most renowned tools for marketing on social media. It gives you the ability tc schedule any kind of posts across any channel you desire. It even lets you specify a posting pattern like daily or weekly.

Buffer also gives you the opportunity to follow up on your posts, seeing which of them were most effective and why.

Sprout Social

This is a complete tool for social marketing which aims in helping managers control their efforts better. It comes with multi-level access, which allows for directional control. It also gives team members at the lower level access to allow them to better delegate and coordinate tasks.

It comes alongside an elaborate analytics platform, post scheduling abilities, and a social listening platform to aid you in a better understanding of how your demographics utilize your chosen platform.

MeetEdgar

This is a tool for scheduling on social media which lets you reuse prior posts. All you need to do is to arrange your posts and schedule content by class. Edgar then goes through and posts your content from every category. The instant it is done going through all the posts you have scheduled; it will begin recycling prior updates.

Hootsuite

This is a tool which is very simple and easy to use. Its simplicity does not compromise how powerful it can be for the average social media manager. It comes with a free version alongside budget-friendly paid options. You can utilize Hootsuite in scheduling posts beforehand on a host of diverse social channels and measure analytics to aid you in having an idea in regards as to how your content is doing.

IFTTT

This means: If this, then that'. Using this, you will be able to merge a range of tools to develop an individual group of instructions. For example, you will be able to set it up to send a tweet whenever you make a new Facebook post. It may be difficult to understand initially, but you can utilize other recipes to make it plug and play. The best part is that it does not cost anything to use.

SocialOomph

At first glance, this solution may not look as complex as a few of the apps above. However, it offers great functionality which makes it worth having a look at. With this solution, you will be able to control a mass of diverse updates at the same time. For example, you will be able to make several blog posts and save them to a text-file. Then, you can upload them to be distributed randomly at specific time-based intervals on the channels you choose. You will also be able to check out intuitive analysis tools and features to aid you in enhancing your audience's engagement.

BuzzSumo

This is another great tool which helps you discover trending, fresh or new content on the internet. With this, you can input a keyword selection or topic and locate a breakdown of some of the trending posts in those classes alongside a list of influencers who are sharing that content.

It is an amazing method of learning new ideas for your social media campaigns and content marketing. It also helps in identifying influencers in your sector who can aid in growing your visibility, reputation and following.

Feedly

This is best recognized as a tool for content discovery. This tool is a content aggregator, and you can utilize it in collecting content from any number of diverse areas, merging your perfect material into one feed that you can go through in your free time.

Although like BuzzSumo, it won't provide you with similar comprehensive metrics, but it will offer you lots of reading material, so you will always have things to post on your social media profiles.

Oktopost

This is a tool designed specifically for B2B organizations. It gives you the ability to schedule content and measure its efficiency, create content to share, and pick up social conversations that are crucial to your organization. It also aids in the management of huge social media teams.

Tagboard

This is a solution for social listening. All you need to do is include a topic, term or hashtag and you will see the discussion regarding that topic in the social scope. It is an advanced method of monitoring things like product and brand mentions, but it is also a helpful tool for generating new concepts on what you should post and how you should engage your followers especially as new trends come up.

Chapter 4:
Top Social Media Platforms

Social media is a platform open to people from various works of life. Are you a business owner, a brand ambassador, or a marketer and what have you? You can leverage the power of social media to your advantage and reach out to a larger target audience.

However, it is essential to know the various social media sites that will enable you to achieve your goals. There are different factors to consider when choosing social media sites to sign up to. Although it is necessary to be part of social media sites with a large user's base, it is more important to belong to one that best fits your business.

Does your target audience use the site? How many of these sites can you manage effectively at a time and how well does the site describe your brand? All of these are things you need to consider equally.

Below is a list of the current top social media sites. You might be familiar with some or all of them. It is advisable that you do a thorough read-through of these sites and decide on the ones that will best fit your brand.

Leading Social Media Platforms Based on The Number of Users

There are five leading social media platforms based on their number of active monthly users, and the first is none other than Facebook. Facebook leads the chart with a staggering figure of 2.2 billion active users monthly. Next in line is yet another popular network with 1.8 billion active users monthly, which is the one and only YouTube. WhatsApp and Facebook Messenger come next in line with monthly active users of 1.5 billion and 1.3 billion respectively. Instagram comes in fifth place having 1 billion active users monthly.

Surprisingly, Twitter and Snapchat didn't make it into the list of the top five as they fell into eighth and tenth positions, respectively while Kik has the lowest figure of 51 million active users monthly. The answer to these three questions will determine the social media platform that will best suit your business.

Who Is Your Target Audience?

Now and then, you may receive ads from various businesses that offer services unrelated to what you require. First, investing in such a business is a complete waste of money, and secondly, most individuals with experience would reason that such businesses need to hire a more competent person to handle their ad targeting.

Reaching out to the wrong audience will only cause you a loss of money and record little or no progress. If you find it challenging to decide the best target audience for your business, the answer to the following questions will show you a way out.

- What is the gender and average age of your target audience?

- What is the average income of your target audience?

- Where are they located?

- Who or what firms do they work for?

- Are they family people?

- Do they own a home?

- What are the challenges they face that require a solution?

- What do they love doing?

- How do they get informed, through the internet or traditional means?

With this, you have a general idea of who makes up your target market. Facebook Audience Insight comes in handy for better profiling of your target market.

Are You B2C OR B2B?

Are you a business to customer (B2C) kind of brand or business to business (B2E) kind? Because it is not yet a common thing for people to visit social media sites whenever they want to make a purchase, it might require considerable effort to get their attention when they would rather scroll over to the next post on their feed unless they are making an impulsive purchase. However, it has been observed that active social media users are the best target market.

The best platform for B2B business where you can promote your business and reach out to the right audience are platforms such as LinkedIn. Here, you can blog about your business, share vital information that will get the attention of people and publish high-quality content.

What Are Your General Social Media Goals?

A good number of business owners, including social media marketers, do not have a clear vision of what they hope to achieve using social media. They keep emphasizing achieving goals without really knowing what their goals are. Chances are you would keep going around in circles without making any visible progress. If you must make sales on social media platforms, then it is necessary that you have a clear vision of what you wish to achieve and work towards it. Always remember that most social media platforms are sites where people go to see things and not to do things; hence, it takes more than just words but action to make a profit off it.

Below are a few social media platforms that would work correctly for both small- and large-scale businesses:

- Pinterest

- Snapchat

- Facebook

- Instagram

- Twitter

- LinkedIn

Top Social Media Platforms for Businesses Facebook

Facebook is the largest social media platform available, with over two billion individuals utilizing it monthly. This makes up a considerable part of the global population. Over 60 million organizations are utilizing Facebook pages and over five million advertisers are actively promoting their organizations on Facebook. This makes it a great option if you want to have a social media presence.

It is easy to begin on Facebook because all kinds of content function properly on Facebook ranging from videos, images, stories and text. However, you need to understand that the Facebook algorithm gives priority to content that triggers relevant interactions and conversations between individuals.

You also need to note that your content must be optimized for mobile because more than 90 percent of the users on Facebook access the application using the mobile app.

It is crucial to use Facebook if your customers belong to any of the following categories:

Seniors: Individuals who are 55 years and above. This is a popular option for this age group because it is where they can view pictures of their family and grandkids.

International markets: As opposed to other websites on social media, Facebook is used globally. It is most popular in Europe and in Middle Eastern countries. However, it is not as popular in Asia.

Small niche markets: Facebook consists of numerous groups where individuals with unique interests gather. If you have a small niche business, Facebook may be filled with groups of likely new clients.

YouTube

YouTube is a platform for sharing videos, and its users watch numerous hours of videos daily. To begin, you can create a channel on YouTube for your brand where you will be able to upload videos for your subscribers to share, like, view and comment.

Aside from being the next largest website on social media, YouTube is frequently recognized as the next biggest search engine next to Google.

Instagram

Instagram_is a social media app for sharing videos and photos. It gives you the ability to share various content like videos, photos, live videos and stories. Recently, it released IGTV for lengthier videos.

If you have a brand, you can create an Instagram business profile. This will offer you in-depth analytics of your posts and profile, and the ability to schedule posts on Instagram with the help of third-party tools. Instagram is ideal if your target market belongs to any of the following:

Millennials: The largest number of users on Instagram are individuals below the age of 25. If your target market consists of this group, Instagram is ideal for you.

Women: According to statistics, men are not as active as women on Instagram. If you sell services and products for women, this platform is the best location to advertise it.

Twitter

Twitter is a social media platform for politics, news, sports, and entertainment among others. Twitter is unique from other social media platforms in that it has a big emphasis on real-time information, which are taking place right now.

Another distinct feature of Twitter is that it supports just 280 characters per tweet as opposed to most of the platforms on social media which have a much greater limit.

Twitter is often utilized as a channel for customer service. As stated by advertisers on Twitter, over 70 percent of social customer service requests take place on Twitter.

There are numerous customer service tools for social media like Buffer Reply, which is available to aid you in managing your customer service conversations on social media.

If your potential customers belong to any of the following groups, Twitter would be a great option for your business:

Teenagers: Like Snapchat and Instagram, it is well-known among teens. Your content has a better chance of going viral among this demographic via re-tweets if it is interactive, funny or thought-provoking.

Millennials: Individuals who are a bit older than teenagers, in the early professional range or just out of college can also be found on Twitter. They took up the trend as teens when Twitter was first released and still use it actively.

LinkedIn

Now, this is more than just a job search and resume website. It has since grown into a professional social site where experts in industries network with each other, share content and develop their brand.

It has equally become an environment for organizations to establish their authority and thought leadership in their sector and draw in talent to their organization.

LinkedIn also provides opportunities for advertisement like sending personalized ads to nboxes of LinkedIn users, improving your content and showing ads beside the website.

If your target markets are in the following groups, LinkedIn is your best option:

Businesses: If you are offering B2B services, LinkedIn is a great location for promoting them. Unlike other kinds of social media, its major goal is to connect with other businesses. For this reason, companies will be in search of services and companies like yours.

High-profile individuals: Some little businesses serve high-profile individuals or executive directors. If this is you, having a profile on LinkedIn is crucial. It shows that you are a professional, serious and established, that is ready to work alongside leaders in the field.

Snapchat

This is a social media application which emphasizes the sharing of short videos and photos, also called snaps, between friends. This popularized the stories format, which eventually branched into other platforms of social media like Facebook and Instagram. Instagram seems to have disrupted the growth of Snapchat and the interest of marketers in utilizing Snapchat for their brands.

If your target market belongs to the following groups, Snapchat is a necessity:

Teenagers: Lots of other groups have not taken up Snapchat yet. Presently, the platform mainly includes individuals younger than the age of 21. So, if this is your target market, then this is an ideal choice. But if this is not the case, this platform consumes lots of time to use.

Reddit
Reddit is also recognized as the internet's front page. It is a platform where users can submit images, questions, and links. They are also able to talk about them and give them an up or down vote.

There are subreddits which cover almost anything you can think of. However, these come with various levels of engagement so it is a great idea to research them to find out if there are popular subreddits you brand can partake in.

Popular Messaging Services

Like social media platforms, there are popular messaging services you should be aware of. Some of these include:

WhatsApp

This is a messaging application utilized by individuals in more than 180 nations. At first, WhatsApp functioned for individuals as a means of communication with friends and family. But slowly, individuals began to communicate with organizations using WhatsApp.

WhatsApp has been evolving to let organizations have an appropriate profile for their business to offer customer support and distribute updates with clients regarding their purchases. For small organizations, it has developed the WhatsApp business application while large and medium businesses have the WhatsApp Business API.

Telegram

Telegram shares a lot of similarity to most of the apps for social messaging and is often recognized for the security it offers as a messaging application.

Brands can utilize it in numerous ways, aside from offering customer support. Brands can develop chatbots for Telegram or use the channel feature offered by Telegram to broadcast messages to an infinite number of subscribers.

All in all, social media is an excellent strategy for digital marketing as long as you prioritize which platforms you use. Don't try to adopt every possible form of social media; instead, do the research and think through which platforms are best for your small business's unique needs.

Chapter 5:
YouTube Marketing

If you are developing plans to start marketing on YouTube, you need to be knowledgeable about it. YouTube has over 50 million content creators producing videos frequently, so your content needs to be unique.

Another issue is reaching and keeping your main audience engaged. Most of the viewers on YouTube do not love advertising that much, so you need to carefully plan how you intend to raise awareness regarding your brand while ensuring you entertain your viewers.

This may seem daunting, but if you use the appropriate approach, it is not impossible to do. Now, before you decide to use YouTube for promoting your business, there are a few things you need to determine first.

Is YouTube Marketing the Best Solution for Your Organization?

YouTube is one of the largest websites around. Presently, it is the second most recognized website globally. And although lots of people don't consider YouTube as a search engine primarily, a lot of individuals use it for just that. YouTube is the next most-popular search engine after Google. What this implies is that this platform offers your business tremendous opportunities.

Because YouTube is a viral platform, it also implies that the competition is enormous. As stated by Statista, YouTube has an upload of 400 hours of video every minute. So, if you desire to attain success on YouTube, you must ensure that you have the resources and time to publish high-quality content consistently. You require an excellent plan for marketing on YouTube.

Another reason that this platform is a great marketing choice is because YouTube is entirely about video. And presently, video marketing is what is trending. Videos have proven themselves continuously as one of the best forms of content marketing with regards to engagement. What is more, although you are developing them for YouTube, that does not imply that you can't use these videos for other purposes.

These videos could suit your other social media profiles. They will also be ideal for your landing pages and websites. That is not all. They can also be a great addition to your email marketing alongside any channels or platforms that you may be utilizing.

As for the problem of video production, it is not as hard as you may think to develop marketing videos. You don't require a massive budget, and you don't have to invest too much in equipment.

In summary, yes, in most situations, YouTube is a good solution for your business. If you are into the sale of products, it is a fantastic method of promoting and showcasing them and all their benefits. If you run a B2B organization, t is a tremendous platform for broadening your reach and getting more leads.

Creating A Marketing Strategy for YouTube

YouTube marketing is like marketing on other social channels. What you need to do first is to develop your strategy. To develop your strategy, you will begin by defining your objectives. Put down the precise targets you want to attain, like:

- Engagement

- Traffic/ clicks

- Subscriber Numbers

Utilize the SMART model to aid you in creating good objectives:

- Specific

- Measurable

- Attainable

- Relevant

- Time-Bound

This will aid in ensuring that your objectives have a deadline, are specific and are possible to do. Of course, you also must be able to measure your progress accurately. At this level of strategizing, determine what your key performance indicators are to aid you in measuring your outcomes.

Understand Your Audience?

You may have a correct sense of your target viewers already, but it is essential to see how they behave on YouTube. Determine if they use their hand-held devices to view videos and the type of videos they are viewing.

Search for useful tools that can help you provide answers to these questions. These tools will give you the ability to ascertain your viewers' habits. They will also give you the ability to make changes to your content.

Understand Your Brand?

If you have plans to market your brand via your channel on YouTube, it is essential that you have a clear definition of what you stand for. You need to also know the way you want to portray yourself to your audience.

Clearly state what you would want your audience to know about your products, services, and brand. Also, make sure this information is passed through your content.

Familiarize Yourself with The Competition

Invest time in viewing and researching your competitor's videos. Doing this will let you see the type of video content they are already creating, the areas they are successful in and areas you will be able to do better.

You can also use this research to attain video inspiration and develop a marketing strategy for your content on YouTube that would make you unique. If you have no idea how to locate your competitors, try searching YouTube with keywords lined with your company. Then look at the videos that relate to your field.

Point Out What Success Seems Like

Before you can create great branded videos, you must determine what success for your organization, and you look like. Is a successful video one that inspires lots of engagement from users or one that pulls in the most viewers?

You will only can create YouTube content that can meet your audience's requirements the moment you have determined what you consider a success.

Follow A Schedule

Consistency is crucial on YouTube if you want to continue growing your channel. Like blogging, the more content you place out there, the higher your chances of getting to a broader audience.

Most successful YouTubers have a rigorous schedule for publishing, and they comply with it. These YouTubers also utilize other platforms of social media in promoting new videos. This ensures that even individuals who are not subscribers of your channel will still have an idea of when new videos will be out.

When creating a YouTube marketing strategy for your organization, put into consideration how you can commit realistically to publishing new content and ensure you follow it.

The instant you have determined your posting frequency, you need to also determine when your videos will be released. Most audiences watch videos on YouTube on weekends and in the evenings. The best time for posting content is early Saturday or Sunday mornings or early afternoons during the week.

During this stage, list out all the upcoming events and holidays significant to your viewers so you will know beforehand possible moments to develop special content.

Kinds of YouTube Marketing Videos

Now that you have figured out your publishing frequency and you know what your goals are, you need to determine the kind of videos you can create on YouTube.

It is crucial to diversify things to keep your viewers entertained and heading back to your page for more. Also, it is a good idea to try out various kinds of videos early, so you know which of them works best for you and which do not.

Below are some concepts to help you begin:

Listicles

These are well-known formats for content, both as media and blog posts. You will be able to develop listicles which pinpoint your services or products such as "the five most creative methods" of using (your services). The listicle can also be informational, educational and entertaining. Don't forget, the list should always be significant to the interest of your audience and your business niche.

Behind the Scenes Videos

YouTube is a social network. One of the methods of humanizing your brand and showing that you are more than just a service or product is by sharing a few behind the scenes videos.

How-To Videos

These tend to perform well when they offer your viewers lots of value. For example, say you were into the sales of electronic devices, you could create how-to videos which show your viewers how to begin using a new device. You can check out blog posts with top performers to get material for these videos, or you can create a plan for a series.

Product Review Videos

This is a fantastic way of showcasing your own services or products. These videos can teach viewers how to utilize specific features, highlighting recent product updates or announcing your company's latest offerings.

Interviews

Interviewing popular influencers and experts in your field is another great method of drawing in new viewers. These professionals will come with their own following, so if they help you in promoting the video as well, they can aid in driving traffic to your channel on YouTube.

Case Studies

Creating video case studies of your customers is another means of promoting your business and services. These case studies don't have to be just about your products alone. They can focus on plans, recent achievements and origin stories of your clients.

How to Manage Your YouTube Channels?

After covering your YouTube marketing strategy, you will want to make an emphasis on managing your channel. Engagement is a major aspect of YouTube, so it is crucial to take time in responding to comments and in driving engagement using other methods.

A great method of managing your account is to utilize a tool to aid in automating the process. Agora pulse allows you moderate your comments in advance, respond to and view comments from the social inbox of your dashboard and observe YouTube for mentions of your brand in comments and videos.

Below are some additional YouTube tips to enhance your views and engagement:

- Go through your comments daily so you can respond promptly.

- Use monitoring to locate other mentions of your brand and find opportunities to engage.

- Ask your viewers questions in your videos. Also, ask them questions in your video descriptions to inspire them to leave comments.

- Utilize the Community tab which you can find in the main page of the channel to post video previews, GIFs, images.

HOW TO MAKE GOOD YOUTUBE VIDEOS

Begin with A Plan

Although making videos on the spot is a great choice for comedy channels, they don't tend to work well for professional ones. Before you begin to film, determine:

- What goal do you want the video to achieve?

- The audience you are targeting these videos for.

- The type of video you want to create.

- Things you will film to achieve the goals of the video.

- Who will you feature in the video?

- The video equipment you will require.

The aim here is to figure out everything and write it down before you begin to film, so that the instant you begin, you can develop the amazing video you thought of initially. The more details you can sort out in advance, the better your chances of getting your viewers intrigued.

Get the Appropriate Video Equipment

There are numerous reasons most brands choose not to create video content, but a major reason is that they believe that they require a host of fancy equipment to make everything look great. Aside from that, they believe they require an expert production crew to run the video equipment. However, the truth is, once you have decided on the kind of videos you want to produce, you will be amazed at how low-tech a few of the crucial video equipment may be.

Now, you will be able to purchase a camera that can capture 4k for a decent price and lots of smartphones today already come with an HD digital camera. Filming can be as seamless as recording a video using your smartphone or camera. You will also require some other tools like lighting, tripod, and a microphone. All of these are easy to use, inexpensive and aid in creating professional videos of high-quality.

Optimize Your Tags, Video Description and Title

The instant you have made your video and began the process of up-loading it on YouTube, one of the initial things you need to do is input the video's tags, description, and title. These are the things search engine crawlers go through whenever an individual carries out a search, so it is crucial to place a lot of consideration into the video tags and keywords you utilize.

When it has to do with your description, consider this as the metadata of your video. Use this section to provide a description of what your video covers, but don't miss out on the chance to add some additional timestamps and links. If you are creating a video about best practices in dog training, don't fear adding a link to your eBook on dog training. Also, if there are specific areas you are confident your viewers would want to go back to or fast forward to, you can add a timestamp in your description to aid them in finding it quickly.

Descriptions have a limit of 5,000 characters, and while it is not a necessity to write a lengthy story, it is not a bad idea to provide your viewers, and crawlers with extra, insightful information to go through.

When inputting video tags, it is a good idea to be honest. Even though it might be tempting to use some tags about a trending, viral subject, the additional views you get as a result of your deceit will only hurt you in the end. If your video deceives viewers into watching, they will not stay around for long, and when YouTube realizes that viewers are leaving your video within seconds, it will negatively affect your search rankings.

You can utilize numerous words in a single tag, but you are restricted to a total of 500 characters, which tends to add up fast. Treat these tags the same way you would any keyword tags on your blog and make efforts to think of all the keywords and phrases your target individuals would utilize in finding a video like yours. If your video has something that is difficult to spell, you can even utilize misspellings deliberately to draw in those searchers who are grammatically incorrect.

Utilize A Custom Image on Your Thumbnail

One of the first things individuals will see after a search is your video thumbnail image, so it is important to choose an image which not only fits the description of your video but also draws attention to it.

After uploading your video, YouTube automatically generates numerous thumbnail images utilizing parts of your video. But, if your account has proper verification and an excellent standing, you will also can upload a custom image of your choice. The instant the video has reached the end of the processing stage, you should be able to view an option to select a custom thumbnail under the section for video thumbnails. Just ensure the file is not larger than 2MB and utilize a 1280x720 resolution for the best outcome.

Requests for Likes, Comments and Subscribers

Although you may find it a bit annoying when individuals ask you to follow, share, subscribe or comment on something online, it is a strategy that has been known to work. In the world of Twitter, requesting users to retweet causes that tweet to be reposted at a much higher rate than tweets that do not. You can also expect to observe similar outcomes when requesting for comments and likes on YouTube.

Obviously, a lot of this is dependent on how great your video is and how you ask, but you will certainly be able to earn additional subscribers, likes and comments just by making a request. This can be of help because the more comments and likes your video gets, the higher the ranking will be on the search algorithms of YouTube.

YouTube stands as the most recognized platform for video hosting on the globe. Your customers, clients, and prospects are all taking advantage of this platform to look for information, which is why it is essential that you grow your presence on this platform.

YouTube Video SEO: Important Aspects

YouTube is one of the core search engines globally. This is one of the reasons why it s an appealing tool for businesses to use in promotion.

Just think about what's possible reaching almost two billion users every month.

What this implies is that if you put in efforts to optimize your videos and you create videos of high-quality regularly, you can drastically enhance the possibility of you reaching a targeted and broad audience.

So, how then can you optimize your videos on YouTube?

There are a host of important elements which determine your social results ranking. A few of them are totally under your control. Some of these include the keywords you utilize and how you utilize them. However, there are other areas you can't exercise control over like how many individuals instantly subscribe after checking out one of your videos.

Below are some crucial ranking factors for videos that you should be aware of. They include:

The Keywords of Your Channel
Utilize the appropriate tags to ensure that YouTube can tell what your channel is offering.

Video Descriptions and Headlines
Research keywords to point out what your audience is searching for and utilize these keywords in your video descriptions and headlines.

Note that, the nearer the keyword is to the start of the headline, the better.

Video Transcript
Adding a video transcript is a fantastic method of ensuring search bots can scrape your videos. It is also perfect for viewers because if they need to check a word's spelling or are unable to hear a video, they will still be able to follow your content.

Watch Time
Your overall video watch time also has an impact on your ranking. The higher the watch time, the better the effect it will have.

Video Tags
Asides from keywords, you must include tags in your videos. To determine the ones that will perform best, you should do proper research beforehand.

Thumbnail Image
This image can be seen anytime your video is indexed. So, you need to ensure it is relevant and compelling.

Number of Subscribers
This has to do with the number of subscribers you have on YouTube. As stated earlier, the amount of people subscribing after checking out one of your videos is also crucial. These subscribers prove that your video was useful to the viewer and offered value.

Marketing Success on YouTube

If you use it the right way, YouTube can be an excellent method of reaching more potential clients and promoting the awareness of your brand. You can ensure your strategy for marketing on YouTube is heading towards success by beginning with these core steps:

- Create a strategy for your YouTube presence beforehand and plan your videos ahead to ensure you regularly publish new content.

- Create various kinds of videos to appeal to a broader audience.

- Put in the effort with each new video to engage with your viewers and subscribers.

- Optimize your videos and channel for YouTube's search engine to improve your reach.

Chapter 6:
Facebook Marketing

Facebook is one of the leading platforms of social media in the world. For this reason, marketing on Facebook has transformed into one of the largest digital channels regarding new opportunities. The platform provides a range of different organic and paid tools which brands can use in putting themselves in front of Facebook's growing user base. Just like any other digital platform, there are a few things you must do if you want to exploit Facebook to gain more leads. Now, let us read on to find out a few of the fundamentals of Facebook Marketing.

Are Your Target Viewers on Facebook?

Before you take the first step and begin checking out strategies for marketing on Facebook. you need to first answer this question - are your target viewers on Facebook?

The answer is most likely.

According to new data, it has been proven that individuals of all ages utilize at least one form of social networking. Younger individuals had the most percentages. Also, women and men use social media in equal proportion.

Additionally, when it has to do with the platform individuals utilize, Facebook is at the top of the list. As of January 2018, 68 percent of Americans utilized Facebook, while Instagram was next with 35 percent.

Irrespective of the age group your target viewers fall in, you will find more users than you need on Facebook.

Now that we have covered this, let us move on to how you begin using Facebook for your promotion.

BUILDING YOUR BRAND ON FACEBOOK

How Can Facebook Aid in Building Your Brand?
The mistake lots of businesses make is assuming that social media platforms, especially Facebook, are just avenues to broadcast the message of your brand to the large number of individuals who utilize the platform. When this fails, lots of these organizations, don't go any further and assume that Facebook does not function for them.

The issue is that this is not the function of Facebook. Individuals do not go on social media platforms to hear you make presentations regarding your business. They don't want boring pitches. Many people go on social media to engage with their friends and the brands they love.

Lots of clients today appreciate brands that make efforts to get to know them on an individual level as opposed to behaving as an impersonal corporation.

Facebook can aid in building your brand by playing the role of an avenue to engage your followers. Offer solutions to their questions and get to know their requirements. When you do this, you develop your brand and inspire brand loyalty.

How Do You Develop A Community on Facebook?

Invite individuals to follow your page on Facebook. Promote your page using numerous platforms which include your newsletters, website, and emails.

Inspire the followers you must engage with your content. When your followers share or like the content you have, it will show up on newsfeeds which all their connections will see as well. This then enhances your exposure and urges more individuals to like your page.

Interact with your followers. Pay attention to the website and promptly respond to their comments and questions. Ask them questions and partake in conversations that show up on your page. Ensure you do not take over the content but instead participate in enhancing engagement.

Why You Should Not Purchase Facebook Likes

If page likes are essential to mastering Facebook marketing, it brings up a valid question: why not just purchase them?

This is a serious issue for lots of people and for others it may seem like an easy and fast way of making your brand look reputable and credible.

Well, the problem is in where these likes come from. Organizations selling likes use fake accounts, click farms or even accounts that have been compromised to get the promised numbers. This implies that there is a low probability of any of these individuals who have liked your page engaging with your content.

Note that, not every post on Facebook comes up on the Newsfeed. When Facebook determines what to add, the algorithm checks out engagement rates precisely. Over time, the absence of comments and likes on your posts due to fake fans in comparison to the number of your overall Page likes, could result in your content not being shown. The average user will equally query your credibility with such differences.

If the future impacts of poor rates of engagement are not adequate to set you straight, note that Facebook has a team that looks out for this kind of distrustful behavior and they will close your page without any form of warning.

How to Create a Facebook Business Page?

If you've decided to create a Facebook page for your business, then you are on the right path. You will become a part of over 50 million businesses globally who are already marketing on Facebook through a page.

Before heading into content publishing and boosting posts via advertising, you need to learn the basics.

Create a Page on Facebook

First, there is one major area to clarify. As you must be aware, most of Facebook consists of personal profiles. But, if you are a business trying to establish your social network presence, you will have to develop a page instead.

Pages are the same as business profiles on Facebook. Pages look like profile pages, but they show precise information only applicable to causes, organizations, and businesses. To connect with a profile, you need to add them as a friend, but when it comes to a business page, you connect by liking the page and becoming a fan. If you make a personal profile for your business as opposed to a page, you have the tendency of Facebook shutting you down.

To begin creating your own page on Facebook, head to https://www.facebook.com/pages/create/. There, you will have the option of choosing from six diverse categories. They are:

- Local Place or Business

- Organization, Institution or Company

- Product or Brand

- Entertainment

- Community or Cause

- Band, Artist or Public Figure

Depending on the option you decide to go with, you will be able to customize the about fields on your page. Wisely select the name of your page. Facebook will allow you to change your URL and name in numerous situations, but it can be a tedious and challenging process.

If you have not done so yet, at this moment, you will be urged to sign into Facebook. To develop a page, you must manage it using your personal account. But your personal information won't show up on the page except if you include it.

Click on Get Started, and you be redirected automatically to your new page. Before sharing with others, Facebook will offer you four building tips for your business page foundation.

Include A Profile Picture

The initial step to providing your Facebook Page with an identity is including a profile picture. This will act as your core Page visual. It will show up in search results along with any of your content that shows up in the news feeds of your users.

Lots of publishers suggest that you create a photo that has a size of 180 x 180 pixels. But, slightly increasing this will aid in maintaining quality, if you fail to upload an image that is square already, you will be asked to crop.

Consider your profile picture as your initial impression and be sure to select something instantly recognizable. If you are a public figure, your best headshot is ideal. Shops or local restaurants may go with an image of their most recognized offering.

Include A Cover Photo

Next, Facebook will request you include a cover photo. This is a vast horizontal image that spans across the top of your page. It should show the identity of your page, and you can update it depending on campaigns, seasons or unique offerings.

To include a cover photo, select the Add a Cover Photo option. The cover photo should have a standard dimension of 851 x 315 pixels. But, if the image is not exact, you will have the option of dragging to reposition the image. Then click save.

To replace your cover photo later, move your mouse over the white camera in the lower right part of your cover image and choose Change Cover. It is also ideal to add a link in the description or a sentence of text if you are advertising a campaign. In doing this, if your cover photo highlights a new product, they can seamlessly head to your product line to purchase.

It can be challenging to find the appropriate balance between a cover photo that is both simple and visual. Try using an abstract pattern or image to draw appeal, or a landscape shot using your product as the core point. Most times, the top cover photos are those that exploit negative space.

Include A Brief Description

A short description is crucial in letting your audience know what you are offering. To begin, all you need to do is select Add a Short Description. You can find it on the welcome menu. Include 155 characters relating to your business. This description will show up both on your search results and page, so ensure it is concise but descriptive. However, don't fear showing some of the personality of your brand.

As an alternative, you will be able to edit your description by selecting 'About' in the left menu. There you will also see the option to add a website, phone number, mission, email and more.

Make A Username for Your Page

The final step on the welcome menu is to develop a username for your page. Your username will show up in your vanity URL or custom Facebook URL to aid individuals in quickly locating and remembering your page. You will be provided with 50 characters to create a name that is not being utilized by another organization.

Create Roles

After the basics, there is a crucial step you need to take before sending the page out to anyone. Remember that Facebook makes business pages unique from standard profiles? One importance of this is that numerous individuals from a company will be able to edit and post via a page without having to share login information. However, this implies you need to elect individuals with various levels of editing access. Page roles become useful here. Above the navigation bar, find 'Settings.'

Then look for 'Page Roles' in the navigation bar on the left. After adding a collaborator, you will have some options for roles which are:

Admin

Can manage all parts of the page. This means they will be able to publish as the page, send messages, delete or respond to comments, produce ads, assign page roles, see the admin who published a post among others. This individual will have similar authority as the individual who created the page, so select wisely.

Editor

They possess similar permissions as admins aside from one major difference. They will be unable to assign page roles to other individuals.

Moderator

These individuals are unable to publish as the page. However, they will be able to send and respond to messages. They will also can delete comments and create ads.

Advertiser

Can develop ads and view insights.

Analyst

They do not have any power to publish, but they will be able to see the admin who published specific posts and view insights.

Live Contributor

If you want to try out Facebook later, the live contributor option will be of help. They will be able to go live from their devices to the page. However, they will be unable to create ads, leave comments, view insights or be able to use any other tools for publishing.

Include A CTA

One of the major significances of creating a business Facebook page is the ability to draw in an audience that you may have been unable to reach if you were using a normal website. Beginning in December 2014, Facebook let pages add a Call-to-action button above the page. Select the Add a Button option on the top of your cover photo to add it.

You will be able to select from a host of options depending on what you need the viewer to do. This could either be to download an application, get in touch, book a service, donate, make a purchase or just get more information.

Verify Your Page

There is a high possibility that you have observed a blue check or tiny gray mark close to the names of a few brands and businesses.

If you classified your page as a company, local business or organization, you could be qualified for a verification badge. This is not compulsory, but it helps in giving your page a sense of authority. This could be specifically crucial for organizations in online services or e-commerce searching to develop trust with possible clients or carry out transactions online.

You could be qualified if you are an admin and your page have a cover photo and profile picture. Head to 'Settings' above your page and find your way to 'General' in the navigation menu on the left. There you will see 'Page Verification' where you will be able to enter your country, publicly listed phone number and language. A Facebook rep will reach out to you with a code for verification.

The blue check badge is only offered to a few celebrities, public figures, and brands. Sadly, you can't request this badge.

How Can You Utilize This Community in Developing Your Brand?

The instant you have a well-known community on Facebook, you need to utilize this group in growing your base and enhancing conversions. You can do this via the following:

First, provide giveaways and unique codes exclusive to your followers on social media.

Secondly, host contests where individuals get coupons which they get for telling stories about the experience they had with your brand or posting images of themselves alongside your product. This inspires individuals to purchase something else while you also spread the reach of your brand via the posts of the participants.

Thirdly, provide inside information about how to get the best out of services or products in your industry. Transform your Facebook page into a significant resource for individuals.

Fourthly, Facebook can be a treasured resource, but it is not just an amplifier for enhancing your message. Utilize this platform in building your brand, and you will find out why social media is popular as a marketing tool.

Making Your Facebook Page SEO Optimized

Your Facebook page is where you begin your marketing efforts on Facebook. Preferably, you want it to be ranking on both Facebook and Google search for your brand name to ensure your prospects and customers can find you with ease.

Then, the instant they have located your page, it should be enticing so individuals will decide to like it. The following are some best practices that can aid you in optimizing your page for both requirements:

Select A Memorable and Descriptive Username

The username of your Facebook page is sometimes referred to as a vanity URL. It is your page's web address. Typically, your page gets a random URL which comprises of numbers. Your username should convey the subject of your business name or page. This is to ensure customers and search engines can locate you in Facebook search and Google. To claim a vanity URL, you must have no less than 25 likes.

Ensure Your About Section Contains Descriptive Keywords

You're about section is your page's core real estate showing text. Ensure it describes your products and business accurately by utilizing what customers are likely to use in search queries. Ensure you add the URL of your website in your description to boost clicks through to it.

Make Sure You Utilize the Right Category for Your Organization

Lots of businesses tend to set their category inaccurately. It can pose a severe issue especially if you need to come up in Facebook's graph search. If your business is a local one, it is important that you pick it as a business type. This is because it will let individuals "check in" at your business. If your business does not have walk-in traffic and doesn't have a use for 'check-ins,' it may be better to select 'Companies & Organizations'.

Optimize the Images on Your Page

Your profile and cover photos are the first things visitors will see when they get to your page. You should have images of professional quality, which should correctly show the feel and look of your brand. Make certain they meet the recommended size requirements, so they don't seem lopsided. The image on your profile should be 160x160 pixels while your cover image should be 851x315 pixels.

Take Advantage of Pinned Posts

Typically, many individuals will only check out your page once. They will like your page and then keep interacting with your posts that show up in their newsfeed but are less likely to check out your wall. Due to this, the main function of your page is to draw people to like your page. Facebook gives admins the ability to pin a post above their page. Make sure this post has a subject that is unique, relevant and has an appealing image.

Utilizing Facebook Groups to Interact with Your Target Market

Although pages are the main tool owners of businesses should be utilizing in marketing their businesses on Facebook, a very efficient add-on strategy in lots of niches and industries are groups. When you use them the right way, groups can be a great traffic source and can result in enhanced authority and engagement for your business.

When you take part in groups owned by other people related to your industry, you will be able to aid in establishing yourself as an expert in your industry. Providing relevant tips and advice can aid you in becoming a relevant member of the group. Also, as individuals learn to trust you, they will want to learn more about your business and you.

However, probably the most valuable utilization of Facebook groups is to create and take part n your groups. Groups offer you the chance to interact with your audience in a more relatable and personal way and let you become a part of the daily conversations of your target market.

Develop a group that allows conversation about any subject that relates to your field. For example, if you are a public speaker, you could begin a group where individuals can discuss or ask questions related to public speaking.

Urging Social Sharing Via the Utilization of Facebook Plugins and Buttons

Your Facebook page and website should seamlessly work together. Often, your marketing funnel will function at pushing traffic from your page on Facebook to your blog or website. But you will always want to ensure you provide your website visitors with a means of sharing or liking your Facebook content. You also want to offer them a means of interacting with your page.

Make sure every piece of content on your website has a share and like button beside it. You will be able to manually add this or utilize a third-party service such as a WordPress plugin to customize your buttons and make the process of adding them seamless.

To offer visitors to your website the opportunity to interact with your page and like it, install the page plugin in your website's sidebar. It is also a good idea to select 'Show Page Posts' to enable visitors to your website to see a preview of the kind of content you normally share on your page.

Getting More of Your Fans to See Your Posts

Lots of page owners typically complain that many of their fans don't see their posts on Facebook. This concern has been addressed by Facebook and they have stated that the inability to see your posts is due to two core factors. Firstly, due to the huge amount of content individuals share daily, there is typically not enough room on newsfeeds of users to display every single post. This leads to a fierce competition for placements in the feeds of users and leads to minimized exposure for organic posts.

The other reason why the reach of your posts has been reduced is because Facebook's algorithm is designed to show users the most relevant content. To determine relevance, there are a host of factors that come into play, including:

- The way a person has interacted with the posts of a page previously in terms of shares, comments, and likes.

- The kind of posts being shared such as video, images, etc.

- The popularity of the previous posts of a page among every user.

The more popularity your posts have, the more they will come up in user's feeds.

To offer yourself the best opportunity of getting it into the feeds of your fans, utilize the strategies below for your organic posts:

Use more videos in your posting strategy. As stated by research, in terms of organic reach, videos are at the top.

Consult your page insights regularly to view the kinds of content your audience loves. Your page insights consist of a vast amount of data on the kinds of content your audience tend to engage with. View the post formats that are drawing in people the most, whether it be links, images, text-only posts or videos. Also, check out the topics your audience seems to enjoy. Also find out the best times, dates and frequency for posting that suits your fans.

When you post promotional content, ensure you add engaging and relevant backstory for the best reach. In 2014, Facebook announced that they would be restricting the reach of posts they deemed "too promotional". These include posts that urged people to enter a con-test, purchase a product or posts that recycled content from ads.

To offer your promotional posts the best opportunity of being viewed, ensure you offer content, which is engaging, as opposed to a plea to visit your website or purchase a product.

Always ask yourself if your audience would find a post entertaining enough to read and interact with it even if they have no plans of pur-chasing your product.

How Often and When to Post

Lots of people who want to post on Facebook always aim to post at the right time on the right day to get peak engagement and reach. But there is no single approach which works for all instances when it has to do with the timing of posts. There has been a lot of research done on the best posting frequency and time, but it is best to utilize this as a starting location for your research. Ensure you check out Facebook insights to find out if these best practices work with your audience.

According to suggestions from research, you might get higher en-gagement when you post on Thursdays and Fridays. Ideal times for posting may differ significantly but posting between 1 pm and 3 pm are great times to begin your testing.

Regarding the frequency of posting, you need to find the middle-ground between informative and annoying. Some brands have been successful in posting 4-10 times daily. For others, once daily or twice a week is ideal. If you post less than two posts weekly, you will not be able to adequately engage your audience for them to retain a social connection with your brand which will cause you to lose their engagement. As a brand, posting more than twice daily can have the same result. What this means is that the right number falls around 5-10 posts weekly if you are a brand and if you are a media company it could be as much as ter times more. This is because news is information individuals tend to engage with every hour of the day.

Utilizing Paid Options to Enhance Reach and Likes

While it is not impossible to get a considerable amount of reach for your posts with the help of free strategies, you may want to use paid options to support your organic strategy. Presently, Facebook utilizes two main options for extending your page posts reach. They are:

Post Boosts

When you boost a post, it will enhance its visibility in the newsfeeds of your users. You can decide to have your posts displayed to the fans of your page, friends of your fans or other individuals who you pick via targeting. Options for the targeting of your posts consist of location, age, and gender. If you want to boost a post, all you must do is select 'Boost' when developing a new post. This setting is also available on previous posts if you need to repost a post that you have published before.

Promoted Posts

You can access promoted posts through your Facebook Ads Manager. To start developing a promoted post, head to the Ad Creator and select Boost your posts. Remember that while this still goes by the name 'Boosting,' you will have more options for budgeting and targeting than just selecting 'Boost' from your page.

Boosting posts is an easy and fast method of extending your post reach, but you can also try promoting your posts as it is an ideal option. Although it is a bit more complex to develop a promoted post, the added control, and targeting of promoted posts usually ensure, they are worth the additional effort.

Chapter 7:
Twitter Marketing

With over 300 million active users monthly alongside a young demographic, Twitter is an amazing platform for lots of marketers.

Beginning a Twitter page for your organization is very straightforward. Anybody can create a twitter handle, fill out their bio, upload their profile image and send out their initial tweet. However, the not so easy aspect of Twitter is to grow your account and transform it into a tool that grows your brand and generates leads.

Growing a real Twitter following requires more than just sending tweets any time your organization is releasing a product or has an event coming up. It also has to do with engaging and interacting with your target audience. Twitter is a very strong tool for marketing. If you can become an expert with this quick-paced site for social networking, you will discover new opportunities to develop your business online.

Why Is Twitter Different

It is not a great idea to use the same approach on all social media platforms. For example, the marketing strategy you use on Twitter is not going to be the same as your Instagram or Facebook marketing strategies. Knowing the way Twitter works and where it fits in in the landscape of social media will determine how you utilize it. Some of the major methods organizations use Twitter include:

- Distributing content and information

- Engaging with customers

- Branding

- Networking

- Management of Reputation

- Pushing Engagement for promotional activities

As you can observe, most of these activities consist of interactions. As opposed to Pinterest or Instagram, it does not necessarily have to do with just broadcasting your content. Twitter feeds off communication.

Now that we have covered the basics let us check a few marketing strategies that you can use on Twitter which will aid you in attaining success.

Steps in Incorporating Twitter into Your Marketing Strategy

It is crucial to determine what you aim to achieve before you plan your Twitter marketing strategy. If you need to get more individuals to check out your content, your objectives should consist of some of these:

- Get leads from Twitter by urging followers to check out your landing page.

- Develop awareness for an upcoming service or product by utilizing Twitter to advertise to relevant leads.

- Develop a positive opinion regarding your services, products, and brands by utilizing Twitter as a tool for PR.

- Offer customer support via one-on-one interactions and relevant content which aids customers in getting the best out of your service or product.

- Develop a community of people with like minds to offer your ideas to innovate a service, product or entire marketing strategy.

- Develop through leadership, interact with like-minded individuals and share your thoughts.

Determine Where Twitter Can Fit into Your Marketing Strategy

Your Twitter plan will possess its own distinct identity in your strategy for content marketing. For example, a few of the things your Twitter strategy may push for are:

Conversions: you may be utilizing Twitter for integrated messaging. This is where you are looking to get a specific action such as an enrollment, subscription or signup.

Traffic: Twitter could be a means of driving traffic to your blog. You could also utilize direct links to landing pages and posts.

Sales: where any kind of tweet, whether blog posts, images, or video have just one aim - which is to enhance sales.

Point Out Your Target Audience
Targeting your audience via Twitter is not easy but very important. But there are lots of ways to locate it, making it less difficult to connect with targeted followers you can advertise your content to.

You also can develop Twitter lists for each section of your audience to monitor who like that content. Below is how you can build targeted lists of individuals you can engage with:

Search Bios for Keywords. There are tools which allow you to search for a user's bio using the target keyword of your content. You are also able to search by location.

Check out Hashtags: Use hashtags relevant to your industry and go through their streams to locate other individuals utilizing them. A session of brainstorming will direct you to the leading hashtags for your marketing objectives.

Follow and Engage: Utilize Twitter list tools such as Tweetdeck or Hootsuite to import your Twitter lists. It will make it less difficult to follow your lists and grow relationships with their members.

Decide on The Best Moments to Tweet

Not everyone is online 24/7. You must determine the periods your followers are online, and that is the ideal time to tweet.

Some things to place into consideration include your location and if your followers are on Twitter at night or during the day among others.

Below are a few tools which can help you decide the best periods to tweet to get peak engagement:

Social Bro. This helps in analyzing your followers' timelines and produces a report that will let you know when you should be tweeting to reach them.

Tweriod: Tweriod will also run a follower's analysis and let you know when they are online alongside the best periods for you to tweet. You will also be able to import these times to your buffer schedule.

Hootsuite Auto Schedule: If you use this tool, this feature will already be aware of the periods of the day your tweets get peak engagement.

Ensure Your Tweets Are Conversational

Most brands tweet in a one-dimensional manner. Their tweets are broadcasts which is not what Twitter is for. Your Tweets should not only be inspirational quotes or headlines with a link or funny statements. They should make way for conversation and communication.

Lots of reputable organizations on Twitter now reply to their customers as opposed to just broadcasting. Below are a few tips that can aid you:

- Tweet questions

- Make sure that no less than 40 percent of your tweets are replies to other individuals.

- When you tweet links, include a line consisting of your opinion to ignite conversation.

- Tweet to your audience directly - as opposed to adding a Blog Post Title and a link, you can instead write: Want to lose weight? Check out this new post: "Blog Post Title (link)"

When you are more conversational, it means an increase in engagement, which also leads to more activity to your account on Twitter in the future. Also, when you are responsive and reply to questions from your audience, it could lead to new customers.

Get Ideas for Your Content

For lots of individuals looking to market their content or services, Twitter is the leading location to find some of the leading ideas for topics. If you're thinking about your next topic or blog post, you can utilize these strategies:

Input Keywords: Input the keywords most relevant to your sector and find out what individuals are talking about. There could be many articles, discussions and a host of others that are taking place right under you. These will let you know what your target audience requires, what is trending, what influencers are talking, etc.

Follow Your Network: Your fans are tweeting about your sector, and they could offer you some relevant ideas. For example, if you see individuals asking numerous questions about a specific strategy for social media, you could write something about it.

Search for Pain Areas: Your prospective clients have issues and questions. They may be engaging on Twitter to find solutions. Keep abreast with things that are occurring to know the questions to respond to.

Select What You Share

There is a host of content on Twitter you can share aside from just text. The platform supports a range of media formats which you can embed directly in your tweet. Some of these include:

Text: These best suit tweets for news, updates, quick facts and asking your followers questions.

Video: Videos are very powerful. If you integrate it in your message, it could help in working wonders by pushing your message in front of the right audience. Include brief but entertaining videos your followers may find useful.

Images: Utilize a picture to enhance your message. It will aid in giving your tweet more impact. Photos stand out better and will help you get more engagement and impressions on your content.

Links: If you have a piece of content which is valuable and is on another platform you can't embed it, although a typical link will work. Include a hashtag to enhance its reach and provide an accurate idea of what the link is heading towards.

Slideshare: Is great for visual data. With the help of slide decks, you will be able to present lots of content in a manner that is easy to digest.

Promoting Your Content

If you use Twitter properly, you can pull in lots of traffic to your site. But, just tweeting your blog post title and a link to your site every time may not give you the results you desire.

You need a bit of creativity when creating tweets to promote your videos, blog posts, and other content. Below are a few ways of getting additional clicks on your tweets:

Leave It Brief: Tweets that do not have more than 100 characters tend to get more conversion. When you are trying to promote something, all you need to do is write a short intro which is adequate for the viewer to know what is waiting for them when they click.

Add Statistics: Individuals love figures and statistics. Utilize Twitter stats that support the argument you are trying to make. It also aids in adding validity to your content.

Add Teasers: Try adding a teaser quote to your tweet. The quote must be accurate and give the users a great idea of what to expect from the post.

Take Advantage of Hashtags: #hashtags are a good way of reaching individuals in your industry that you are not presently following. Use popular industry hashtags to do this. You can also use branded hashtags and inspire others to use it too.

Utilize Mentions: If your post mentions any industry influencers or publications, make sure you mention (@) them when promoting. If the content is good enough, there is a high chance they will also share it. This will help you reach their audience.

Request for A Share: If you want retweets, this is a great practice. All you must do is ask your audience to aid you in retweeting a post. Tweets requesting for RTs have a higher tendency of obtaining them.

Promote Your Tweets: If you are looking to get more exposure, then Promoted Tweets will help in attaining it. With just a little investment on your part, you will be able to achieve this. They are not difficult to create and can aid in bringing you a huge amount of traffic.

Creating A Tweeting Schedule

You need to have a scheduled time for posting tweets on Twitter. Your schedule for tweeting should show what you plan on tweeting and when. Your strategy should put down things like when you will be tweeting links to your new posts alongside other updates.

It's a good idea to add this into your total content strategy, especially if you tend to publish content across numerous platforms such as YouTube, a blog, etc. A major benefit of having a tweeting strategy in place is that you can avert errors like just tweeting links to recent blog posts once. Generally, this is one of the major errors brands on social media make, but it is especially worse on Twitter.

The issue with tweeting links to your content out just once is that lots of people won't see it. You must give your tweets time intervals to enhance their visibility, and to make sure that as many individuals as possible can view your content. The next question would be when should I tweet? You need to find out when your audience is most active and spread your tweets within those periods. This will ensure there is a higher possibility of people seeing your Tweets.

Set Milestones and Goals

If you don't have measurable goals you want to reach, your marketing strategy is missing a crucial factor. In the absence of milestones, goals, and objectives, you have a higher tendency of making similar errors many marketers and businesses make with marketing on social media.

Lots of businesses don't exactly know if their efforts on social media are functioning or not. A big reason behind this is that organizations do not monitor their activities and neither have they set any objectives for what they intend to achieve on Twitter.

Instead, organizations just send out content and hope something will happen to enhance their brand. The strategy of publishing and hoping is not enough. First, you will have to set some goals and objectives on Twitter such as:

- Develop an engaged audience

- Monitor and enhance the reputation of your brands

- Respond to the complaints of your customers faster

- Draw more traffic to your site

- Generate Leads

- Network with influencers and bloggers

Next, you will create accomplishments that go alongside those objectives such as:

- Enhance Retweets and Mentions by 20 percent

- Keep your rate of response higher than 90 percent

- Ensure your answer is not more than 10 minutes

- Generate no more than 10 leads from Twitter monthly

- Increase traffic from referrals on Twitter by 30 percent

Ideally, all goals should come with a stated deadline. This could be monthly, weekly or quarterly or whatever works best for your organization. Utilize website analytic tools like Google Analytics and a social management tool to measure your activity and monitor the progress of your goals.

If you follow these steps, you will go further than just creating a Twitter account and following random individuals hoping you get a follow back. Try to emphasize utilizing Twitter to engage and develop your brand.

Verify Your Account – Why You Should Verify

If you have a verified Twitter account, it separates your brand or organization from the shady ones that have been created and offers you credibility. However, you need to meet specific criteria when applying for verification. These are:

Ensure Your Profile Is Updated

You need to ensure all your profile information is updated and accurate. This consists of your header picture, profile picture and bio.

Phone and Email Verification

Next, you must confirm and verify your email address and phone number. You can find the options to do both of this in the Settings and Privacy option.

Let Your Tweets Be Public

To get a verified account on Twitter, you need to set your tweets to public. Next, ensure your profile has to do with your business. This implies that having a stock image on your handle could prevent you from getting verification.

Apply for Verification

Donald Reammsei

The instant your profile is ready, you will be able to apply for verification via the request verification form on Twitter. Ensure you make available any supporting documents or URLs of websites that could aid your cause in your respective industry.

If you are trying to verify a personal account, you may need to submit an ID card issued by the government. Then a group of moderators will aid in reviewing your profile before a decision is made. If your verification request is not approved the first time, you are able to apply again after 30 days.

Chapter 8:
Instagram Marketing

It did not appear like Instagram was anything special when it first made its way into the social media scene in 2010. Instagram had a lot in common with the then available social media platforms. It contained pictures of different foods, pets, and selfies.

Eight years after 2010, Instagram is no longer a platform for just posting pictures. It is now a tool for carrying out full-scale marketing.

When a look is taken at a log of the latest features on this platform, it is evident that lots of instruments that are beneficial to businesses have been added to Instagram in the last 12 months. Some of these tools are fresh methods of pushing traffic on Instagram, advanced analytics, and Instagram posts that are shoppable.

It doesn't matter what sector of the economy you find yourself in, you will not regret having a strong Instagram presence. However, if you must get in front of others, it is vital that you have a perfect understanding of Instagram, as well as your target audience on this app. You should also know the types of content that generate the most views, how to get your KPIs and metrics tracked, and how to have a strategy for Instagram stories.

Why Instagram Marketing Is Key to Ecommerce Success

Virtually everyone is aware of how amazing it is to share videos and photos with friends and loved ones on Instagram. That, however, is not all that Instagram is about. It is an excellent tool for e-commerce.

Why is this so? Well, the simple reason for this is that Instagram has a very visual format. As a result of this, it offers lots of opportunities to e-commerce businesses that are interested in showing off what they have. This can be done through Instagram stories, videos, and photos. Lots of businesses are now aware that a strong presence on Instagram is an excellent complement for e-commerce marketing.

Tips for Instagram Marketing That You Should Know

Optimize Your Bio

In addition to your username, website URL, and business name, there are 150 characters offered by your Instagram profile for inputting your bio.

Your bio gives you the privilege of making a first impression. It is also a chance to tell people about your business. With your bio, you should be able to tell people who you are, as well as the services you offer. This is in addition to giving out information about the Identity of Your

Brand. With just 150 characters, doing this might not be so easy. This, therefore, makes it vital that you have a copy that is:

- CLEAR: Make use of simple and short words. Also, your texts should have line breaks.

- CONCISE: Emojis can help you develop a personality for your brand.

- COMPELLING: With a call to action, it is very easy to let visitors know their next line of action.

Select the Right Profile Picture

Your profile picture creates a first impression. Visitors to your page notice it before going on to your bio. As a result of this, a business Instagram account will have to make use of its logo as its profile picture. Every logo must be untouched by the circle which Instagram is known for. It should also be clear. By zooming out, you can fix a logo that has a square appearance.

Build Consistent Instagram Aesthetics

If there's one thing that's difficult about making your Instagram feed have a great look, it's getting your pictures to look good when placed together. It is essential to look beyond just posting a picture and look at your entire Instagram feed - how do your photos look beside each other? These tips should help

Select A Color Scheme

Having a steady color scheme meant just for Instagram feeds is important. The result of this is there will be an effortless blend between the colors throughout your feed. You may decide to make your feed warm and comfortable, cool and dark, or colorful and bright.

Irrespective of what combination you intend using, with a color palette that is consistent, it becomes easy to add branding to your Instagram feeds.

Focus on Lighting

As far as aesthetics and duration are concerned, lighting is of the utmost importance. Picture any upscale magazine that you enjoy reading. Irrespective of what is being discussed - the choice of colors, as well as the lighting are key attractions. Your Instagram should maintain a consistency in these areas for a more pleasing aesthetic.

Your Goals Should Be Clearly Defined

In the absence of any created goals, there will be no way to tell if your investment in Instagram marketing is yielding a profit. The first step in the creation of goals is selecting the best yardstick for gauging success. This falls into two classes:

- "Vanity" metrics (shares, likes, followers, comments)

- "Business" metrics (traffic, revenue-gen, engagement, reach)

With vanity metrics, you can estimate how your content is faring and how your audience view your content. With vanity metrics, you can also know how competitive your presence is on Instagram.

Business metrics will give you a view of social media's contribution to business in the big picture. They are both important in different ways. Also, they must be considered before setting up a Business In-stagram.

Create Engaging Content
Engaging content attracts an audience. It drives people to share, click, and comment. You cannot get an individual to take any action if you can't get them to give you attention. There are lots of methods which will get people's attention and focus. Some of them are:

Behind the Scene Shots
This content format is used to introduce the individuals that serve as your business's backbone. With behind the scene videos and images, the humane side of your brand is revealed. This makes followers re-alize that collaboration has a role to play in driving your business.

It is also okay to make posts that publicize the profile of some of your executives, show employees at work, and show what your office looks like. Whatever helps outsiders have an idea of what is going on inside.

Space Out Your Content

This can be the most challenging part of creating an attractive Instagram feed. It is important that you are aware of just where each photo should be, as well as how to have a planned feed that helps all photos blend together.

Your aim should be to develop a depth of field, just like in the case of photography. You might need to separate busy photos from each other and keep them closer to minimal photos to get the right balance.

Keep Things Consistent

To ensure that your feeds have a natural flow, it is vital that you take the right approach when correcting your photos. The implication of this is that you can't work with just one filter. However, making use of just a few filters will be great.

Do you like warmer tones? Regardless of what style you use in editing, ensure there is a consistency that will let you maintain a good flow. The use of just a tinge of one filter style can help your brand in more ways that you are aware of.

Quotes and Text-Based Images

A lot of people enjoy going through quotes that they have a good understanding of. This, therefore, makes quotes a tremendous and relatively effortless way to build engagement. You should develop text-based material that takes advantages of:

- Quotes made by people of influence in your industry

- Facts that are specific to an industry

- Satisfies customer reviews

Daily Hashtags

With daily hashtags, it s easy to streamline your content. This can also help you develop a theme which can keep your audience expectant. It also plays a role in helping you come up with ideas.

Try developing some classy hashtags. An example of this is #tbt (Throwback Thursday), which is known by lots of people. You can also go ahead and develop something entirely new. It could be related to the business you are involved in.

Master the Little-Known Features and Hacks

Are you aware that it is possible to:

- Alter the color of fonts, as well as words so your text can be unique?

- Hide your story from specific individuals?

- Include line breaks in your bio to make it less difficult to go through?

Instagram is rich in features and is suitable for the creation of content that is unique. If you can master some of these relatively unknown features, you will be able to get the best out of Instagram.

Partner with Relevant Influencers

If you are in search of a tried and tested way to give your business the right level of attention, you can explore a partnership with an influencer that is relevant. This will have to be paid for.

It is important to note that influencer partnerships vary in some ways. There are lots of questions that you must provide answers to while trying to get an influencer. Some of these questions are:

- "Do I share the same values, personality, and aesthetic beliefs with the influencer brand I am considering? "

- "Have they partnered with any brand and product which share some features with my brand?"

Make Use of Great Headings

As far as engagement is concerned, captions can be said to be as vital as the videos or images that they augment. With the right caption, you can make your brand's personality known, as well as entertain your audience all at once.

The ideal captions can be read easily, is clear and straight to the point. As a matter of fact, the ideal captions save the reader the time of trying to decipher them. They can be understood effortlessly.

You must know the voice of your brand, as well as your audience if you want to achieve this effect. If you know your audience, you can always have content that interests them. Also, knowing your brand voice will help with consistency.

Make it a practice to try out some copywriting tactics (e.g., ensure that words that are considered most important make it to a caption's beginning). It is equally important to practice these techniques.

Choose Hashtags Wisely
If you are looking to get attention, hashtags cannot be overemphasized. When correctly made use of, a hashtag can direct lots of visitors to your brand, posts, and profile. However, a misleading hashtag, especially when irrelevant or used excessively can bring about lots of negative results.

The reason for this is if a user comes across anything they do not like after following a hashtag, they can always click on the option "Don't Show for This Hashtag".

According to Michael Aynsley, Hootsuite editor, this feature was created to tell the Instagram algorithm the kind of content a specific user like. However, if Instagram flags too many of your posts, it is assumed that your content will come up less or not at all. When making hashtags, you need to consider the following:

- Stay relevant, do not try to stuff hashtags

- Stay specific, have a target audience.

- Do not mistake the meaning of the hashtag for something else

- You must be concise - when a hashtag is short, it is easily re-membered.

Get on The Explore Tab

If you want to build the visibility of your brand in the shortest time possible, make use of the Explore tab. With the Explore tab, users can locate content that is curated as a result of the actions that they took in the past. The implication of this is that Instagram is aware of your activities. It is, therefore, able to push related content to you explore tab.

Also, Instagram gets content from accounts which have something in common with those you follow. It is all dependent on pattern recognition and data, and it leads to the question: what are the ways to get your content onto the explore tab? Although there are no specific methods, a lot can be done to give yourself a good chance:

Know Your Audience

Who is your target audience? What are their interests? Who is the people they currently follow on Instagram? To discover what drives engagement with your audience, make use of reverse engineering.

Make Use of Hashtags

One straightforward way to get people to discover your content is to make use of hashtags. When you use hashtags, it makes it easy for your content to be discovered. This is one reason all marketers should make use of them

Encourage Engagement

As the likes, comments, and shares of an Instagram post increases, the likelihood of these posts appearing on the explore tab of your target audience increases.

To get better engagement, you should geo-tag your posts and mention other accounts that are relevant while writing your caption. As the relevance of your post increases, there will be an increase in the likelihood of you compelling more action from your audience.

Target the Right Audience with Ads

Do you find yourself in a space that is very competitive? You might need to make use of Instagram ads to promote your brand.

There are five formats for ads on Instagram: photos, videos, canvas story ads, story ads, and carousels. The feeds or story of your target audience has each format incorporated into it. This, therefore, makes it difficult to omit.

Although it is possible to build your Instagram presence without spending money, you can be confident that it will take a long while. If you want to get things done faster, you should take advantage of ads.

How to Use Instagram Stories for Business?

Making use of Instagram stories to carry out business transactions is currently an essential part of all marketing strategies on Instagram. Doing this can aid you in interacting with customers, and in pushing engagement.

It is not very easy to find ideas for Instagram stories and decide on what you will post. Well, if you require inspiration, below are ways in which businesses make use of Instagram stories.

Promote Your Products And/or Services

Instagram stories have an organic tapping progression. This makes it an excellent place to grow expectations around fresh products.

To do this, simply ensure that your story is packed with various photos of one product at all possible angles, in various environments, and with various people. Once done put a promo code. Once you have enough followers, you'll be able to add clickable links to your Instagram stories.

Build A More Engaged Community

Just like regular posts, when you make use of Instagram stories to promote a business, make it a combination of promotional, light-hearted, and fun contert. Instagram stories is not a very serious environment. This, therefore, makes it a good place for every type of post.

Run an Instagram Stories Takeover

A very simple way to make use of Instagram stories is to get an individual to present your story or get involved in an Instagram stories takeover.

With a frequent guest segment, you can spice up your use of Instagram stories. If you want to give it a try with your business, feel free to select anyone from your firm to carry out an everyday life story. You can also swap stor es with other businesses in your sector.

Track Your Performance with Instagram Analytics

One straightforward way to stay on course while looking to achieve your marketing targets for Instagram is understanding and tracking your analytics.

Irrespective of what you are trying to track - reach or general engagement, there are ways to get it done quickly. With a business profile, it is easy to access Instagram Insights. Making use of Instagram Insights can help you get all the information you need from a dashboard

Chapter 9:
Abide by these Social Media Marketing Laws

The introduction of social media marketing into the digital industry about a decade ago has brought about significant changes in the marketing process. This has made marketing a lot easier and helps one reach a broader audience within a short period with less stress involved.

If you don't yet understand what social media marketing all is about, the best way to begin is to get acquainted with the basic rules and play by them.

Do you want to grow your business or brand, reach a larger targeted audience and turn them into potential customers? If yes, then here are ten fundamental laws of social media marketing every social media marketer must know and abide by to achieve their desired result.

The Law of Prioritizing Quality
This law encourages you to pay more attention to those followers of yours who show more interest in what you have to offer than those who care less. Rather than trying to build a broader audience of

uninterested followers, create quality content and provide quality products that will keep your active followers interested in your brand or business. Always keep in mind that quality supersedes quantity.

Never underestimate the power of a well-written article. You would rather have one carefully written article than a thousand shabby ones. Do not rush when creating your content, give it the attention and effort it requires and never hesitate to ask for external help if need be.

The Law of Empathetic Listening

If you want to have a stronger impact on your audience, learn to interact with them. Find out which trending topics or subjects' matter to them and include those in your content. By doing this, you keep your followers engaged and active on your page and give them reasons to continually come back for more. It is important that you pay attention to the preferences of your audience and give them what they want. Interact with them in the best way you can, and you are good to go.

The Law of One-Point Focus

Be specific in the products or the services you provide, avoid handling too many different things at the same time. This will limit your efficiency and reduce the quality of your content as you are stretched amongst different things, and finally scare away your customers because you come across to them as confused and unserious.

Choosing a specific niche to operate in gives you a better chance at succeeding than venturing into different unrelated niches. Your area of specialization will determine your customers; it is, therefore, your duty to choose carefully. When the need to look for external aid arises, do not give it a second thought. Always offer your customers and other potential customers the best.

The Law of Adding Value to Voice

The importance of promoting your brand or business can never be overemphasized. However, it is necessary to pay attention to other essential things that will help your brand grow. Ensure the quality of your products and services do not depreciate while you are putting in so much effort at promoting your brand. Post entertaining content occasionally that will excite your audience. Appreciate your customers by giving them incentives such as giveaways, discounts on your products and services, and more. This will go a long way at increasing their loyalty and even attract more potential customers.

Continuous promotion of your products or services without giving your audience something new to chew on might eventually leave them uninterested in your content causing you a massive setback.

The Law of Reciprocated Efforts

This is another law every social media marketer must apply for a better outcome. When a brand or an online influencer with a large followership shares your content on their platform, it is necessary that you reciprocate the favor. Reciprocating widens your reach and promotes your page even more. Therefore, if you wish for your content to be shared by brands and influencers with a large audience, you must also be willing to do the same. Never assume that a big brand or influencer does not need your promotion, it would be selfish of you to expect them to continually share your content without reciprocating. This could cause them to lose interest in your business and focus on those who understand the principle of reciprocation. With the high rate of competition in the world today, applying this law will help you stand out amongst so many similar brands. Your inability to play by this law might cause your business to suffer setbacks or slow your progress.

The Law of Patience
Succeeding at social media marketing requires excellent patience and doesn't happen by chance. To excel at this, you must be willing to put in great effort and time to get the best result. The world is now highly competitive, and mediocrity can barely survive. This is even more reason why you must take your time at creating quality content that will speak to your audience.

Think of social media marketing as an upcoming examination, and your grades depend on the amount of effort you put into your studies. Mere opening of your books and staring at them cannot give you the good grades you desire. This is also applicable to social media marketing as you can only excel when you give it your best and do not quit after a short while.

A lot of businesses throw in the towel and walk away shortly after they venture into social media marketing due to slow progression, forgetting that this process takes time to produce positive results.

The Law of Compounding

This law is the most important of them all. Quality content has a way of reaching out to a broader audience. This is because people value quality more than quantity and do not hesitate to share when they come across it. Therefore, it is essential to give it your best when creating content.

A subscriber who appreciates the quality of your products or services on YouTube might be prompted to tweet about it on Twitter or make a post on Facebook and Instagram encouraging others to visit your channel without being paid to do so. As a result, you may experience an increase in the number of subscribers and views on your post which will eventually translate into financial success.

The Law of Influence

According to this law, it is essential to have a good relationship with brands and online influencers who have many active followers and customers. If they find your content compelling enough, they might decide to share it with their followers exposing you to a broader audience of potential customers.

TIP: Choose the influencers you would like to work with and promote them on your platform. This will enable you to connect with their audience, creating a type of bond between you two. Note that there is always a unique audience for the products and services you offer; however, you must figure out a way to get across to them.

The Law of Acknowledging Everyone

Keep pride and arrogance far away from you. Never ignore a person who reaches out to you. Treat this with the utmost importance and show respect to whoever is involved no matter how occupied you are.

Endeavor to appreciate any post a person makes about you or if you are tagged in a positive post. Merely saying "thank you" or responding politely will give your followers a sense of importance, making them loyal fans. This is a fundamental law you must play by as nobody likes to be ignored.

Your approach towards your social media relationship should be like that of a physical one. People will stay loyal to you when you appreciate their efforts towards your growth. Instead of treating them as a mere pawn that is of little value, show them love and let them know how much you value their effort.

The Law of Accessibility

Keeping your audience engaged is always of great importance. Do not make the mistake of continually ignoring your audience or not interacting with them. This will kill your brand faster than you can imagine.

When you publish a post, stay on it and respond to comments and questions as much as you can. Social media is a two-way street, and communication is key to growth. It is much easier to forget businesses or brands that are not easily accessible.

To avoid stagnancy or decline in the growth of your business, prove to your audience that you are readily available for them. Let your actions speak for you. Do your best to reply to every direct message sent to your brand page inbox within 24 hours as it is rude and unprofessional to ignore them. Always be available to respond to the needs of your customers.

Although a lot of businesses are aware of the benefit of social media marketing, only a few have a deep understanding of how it works and take advantage of it.

Never forget that to succeed at social media marketing you must consistently create posts and offer products and services that appeal to the desires of your clients. However, to achieve this, it is essential to apply the right approach. Design effective strategies that will help you reach your desired audience and never hesitate to make amends or request for external help when the need arises.

Chapter 10:
Convert Followers to Customers

Now that you have a decent number of fans and followers on your social media page, and have followed all the provided steps, you're probably wondering, "How do I convert these followers into actual customers?"

This is a question lots of businesses on social media tend to ask themselves later.

It does not have to be complicated if you know what to do. Below are a few tips that will make this process seamless and provide you with the customer base you require.

Analyze Every Social Channel

If you want to convert followers and fans into customers and make connections, you need to know which social media platform supports your efforts the most.

Start by analyzing the available information you have for every social media channel. Some questions you need to figure out include:

- Which of your social media platforms has the largest audience?

- Which of them has had the most success in keeping your audience engaged?

- Which of them has helped in generating the most business leads?

- What are your followers saying regarding your business on social media?

- What are your followers saying on social media generally, and how can you integrate this into your business?

While analyzing your social profiles is crucial, it is also important to keep an eye on your niche and industry. What are the significant conversations taking place and how do they identify with your business strategy?

To go further and inform the decisions you make, you can utilize data from Twitter, Facebook, and Google Analytics.

Using this data, you can place focus on the most important social media websites, then adjust your content strategy before creating posts that complement that strategy.

Understand Your Target Audience

If you want to be successful in social media marketing, you need to point out your target market clearly. Carry out research and create a customer persona that will aid you in this. What age range does your target market include?

Let us assume you have pointed out your target market, and they are in the age groups of 17 – 25. You have a Facebook page, which is ideal because over 80 percent of that audience has a profile on Facebook.

But you are not efficiently making use of your profiles if you are not using Snapchat, YouTube, and Instagram.

While it is crucial to be on as many channels as possible, your target audience will determine the level of input you require on each one. For those who are only marketing to individuals over the age of 50, it is not effective focusing your marketing efforts on Tumblr and Snapchat.

But a few of your businesses may have a broader range of services and products which converts into a more diverse target market. You will have to utilize every social channel in a different manner, based on the users you want to reach.

If you are trying to sell g asses to a 60 year old, Snapchat will not be the channel for this. Ensure your promotions are relevant for the social channel you are utiliz ng.

Concentrate Your Social Media Efforts

Now that you are aware of which social media platform has the most importance to your business, and you have a clear definition of your audience, you need to concentrate your efforts.

Except you have a social media team managing your social media, you will need to put in a lot of effort yourself. There is no benefit to your business if you have a presence on five websites and ignore them all until, they die off.

It is best to concentrate on 1 or 2 websites and work with those. Once you are successful, you can move onto other sites. You can also use your audience metrics to aid you in pinpointing the social media channel you want to head to.

Let's presume you are doing well on Facebook and one of your targets is 60 years old; you will want to consider a channel more popular and significant to individuals around 60 years and above. It is also crucial that irrespective of the social media platform you are using, that you offer quality content that urges them to head to your website. If your content is very engaging, your level of success is going to be high.

For example, let us assume you are in the food niche. Develop an exciting and relevant blog post on the best Japanese meals. Add a link to a significant landing page on your site. Ensure the link is related to the content and not just any page on the website.

You can also use the blog post as a means of getting clients to sign up to your email list. The more often you keep in touch with clients, the more likely they will consider your business when they have the need for a product or service you sell.

Have A Thorough Understanding of The Chosen Platform

The instant you know the platform that works perfectly for your business, you need to learn how to utilize that platform efficiently. Using the information, you have amassed, you will have the ability to develop a strategy around specific content. However, you will be unable to utilize the same content on all platforms.

Remember, what works on Twitter may not work on Facebook. The same is also applicable to your Instagram and YouTube posts.

Your content needs to have the same focus but with different strategies. Below are a few examples:

- A blog post on LinkedIn on how particular meal ingredients could be harmful to your health which links back to your page of healthy food ingredients you sell.

- A picture of healthy meals with their ingredients on Instagram which links back to the post of healthy food ingredients.

- A Twitter post about your most recent meal using hashtags about trending topics you have researched.

- A link on Facebook to your blog post alongside a call to action to share and like your page.

Promote and Sell

You can also convince fans and followers to buy your products. You can do this using sales exclusives and deals.

For example, post coupons exclusive to your audience on Facebook. It is not difficult to provide coupon codes but are only announcing to fans or followers of your Facebook page.

Customers enjoy feeling special, and Facebook gives you the ability to make them feel so. Discounts exclusive to followers of your page will be more cherished by your clients. This could not only enhance the number of followers you have but also, aid in turning individuals who like your page into buyers.

The promotion does not have to be an immediate purchase or sale for a limited time. There are studies which show that 40 percent of individuals will like a page on Facebook if it means you will provide them with a discount on their subsequent order. Another choice is to send a coupon to blog subscribers in a newsletter. While selling products at a lower price, you will end up with lots more sales as a result of the promotion which could also result in continuous sales.

Think Past Your Organization

To establish a presence that clients will keep coming back to and consider when shopping, it is a good idea to think past your own content.

For example, you can use Facebook to link to posts that will relate to the interests of your audience occasionally, and not only link to your organization's page.

On Twitter, you can post quotes that inspire your audience, or provide questions to your audience using hashtags like "What is the biggest frustration for people when trying to eat healthily?" Twitter is also a means for people to find news, so you can develop tweets using trending pop culture topics or sharing content of influencers that are significant to your organization.

Engaging and fun content will bring you a broader social media presence and will ensure you always remain first in the minds of clients. Consider channeling your effort in developing a presence that goes beyond sales. Some professionals have recommended that you follow an 80/20 rule. You will focus only 20 percent of your posts on sales and content, while the rest should be on more general information your audience would find relevant. Find a middle ground that works for you and your organization.

Do You Have Loyal Fans?

Loyal fans translate into loyal customers. But, for a follower to transform into a loyal follower you as the owner of the business must show loyalty first.

Frequency and consistency will help show your loyalty. To get this done, post content in a consistent manner. Whether this implies posting on precise days every week, or an exact number of times every day, your followers will begin to look forward to your messages.

It is okay to take a break but be sure you inform your followers about it. For example, if you are going on vacation, tell them and let them know you will miss them and look forward to sharing pictures and content when you come back. You can also let them know that you will be in touch intermittently during your absence. This shows that you respect their loyalty.

Similarly, to show you care, inform them that their thoughts are important to you. When they respond, leave a comment. Prove that you care about them continuously, just the way you do when you interact with your actual friends every day.

Provide Your Followers with Exclusive Deals
Make your customers feel special. Providing your followers with exclusive deals will ensure they come back continuously. These deals do not have to be complicated, instead, keep them fun and simple.

For instance: "20% off all our packages if you purchase today, exclusive to our followers on Twitter. Send us an email and mention you saw this post." You can even begin a deal of the week. This will ensure followers keep checking in and coming back for more.

Be Responsive and Active

When you have attained lots of followers and reached some sales objectives using your presence on social media, you should continue being active and responding to your clients.

One of the most important aspects of social media marketing is to post frequently and keep being relevant to your followers. You can utilize tools to schedule posts and maintain a consistent posting presence. Irrespective of how you achieve it, these frequent updates will leave your name in the minds of your potential clients and existing clients.

Also, you need to respond to your clients. You need to respond to any comments or questions on your website quickly. Any customer or potential client will value an honest and fast response, so ensure you are available to those who reach out to you using social media.

Facebook users expect a speedy reply to their messages. Spending too much time before you respond or failing to respond will hurt your image, and one bad communication can leave lasting adverse effects.

On the bright side, you can also use positive comments and interactions of clients to promote your business further. Spend extra time each day updating and monitoring your presence on social media.

Invite Them to Something Personalized and Entertaining

Offer your followers some VIP attention. For example, invite all your followers on Instagram to a live video feed where you will be responding to their questions in your area of expertise.

Inform them that this is just for your followers on Instagram and you will respond to only a specific number of individuals. You can do something similar on Facebook via your fan page or on Twitter using hashtags. Be sure to inform them that you will be available to provide solutions to their problems.

You can also allow your followers to submit questions in advance through direct messaging, and only those that you receive within a specific time will get a response. This will also ensure your event goes smoothly as you do not have to wait for anyone to join the live feed to ask a question.

Promote Your Audience

This is an excellent method of building credibility, giving back and strengthening your relationships. As soon as you have developed a good relationship with your followers, they will transform into customers.

Choose a day of the week on Instagram to promote one of your followers. This does not imply you should mention five followers and do a photo-mix of them. This is neither promotional nor personal. Instead, choose some followers that you always engage with and mention why you value their input.

On Facebook, there is an application that can help with this. You can include the fan of the week application to your fan page.

Allow Your Clients And Customers to Have A Say

Pay attention to the encouraging things clients and customers say about your products and business. One method of doing this is by asking, perhaps at the end of a coaching call, "What is the most important thing you learned today?" Then also ask, "Can I share your takeaway on Twitter or Facebook?"

Sharing testimonials reminds your followers about the services and products you offer. But, further than that, it proves that others have found your products or services to be useful.

Try Out Paid Ads on Social Media

Spending on social media applications is a fantastic method of developing a targeted following. Almost every core social media channel which includes Instagram, Facebook and LinkedIn, provide paid ads.

You can use these to enhance your content views, reach, engagements and clicks. You can get the best of your investments with offers and reconstruct past posts to target possible clients. In doing this, you will be able to get new subscribers, followers and potential leads for the future.

The best aspect of ads is the ability to get precise with your demographic targeting. You will be able to tailor a variety of ads to various personas with fantastic accuracy. This enhances the possibility of targeting more business clients.

Offer Customer Service on Social Media

Fantastic customer service is often the deciding element that makes customers pick one business over another to purchase from. This is because your efforts are always displayed publicly.

More than 80 percent of customers utilize social media to speak directly to businesses, and it also happens to be their method of preference for customer care. Replying quickly to resolve the queries of your customers can aid in enhancing trust and significantly boost your reputation.

Offering amazing customer support on social media is a fantastic method of enhancing business via word of mouth marketing. What is more, you will be able to develop positive press for yourself, which can have a positive impact on your customer procurement on social media.

Utilizing social media in promoting and marketing your business can take a lot of time, but the rewards are tremendous. Taking time to develop your strategy before you leap can provide you with the results you desire.

Utilize all available data, understand your channel, develop content significant for it and your followers, and ensure that they remain responsive and active.

Don't get discouraged when you reach your first hurdle. Analyze and make changes as required, and social media will be a useful addition to your business strategy.

Chapter 11:
Proven Social Media Secrets

In the digital world today, your availability on social media is of great value to the growth of your business. Your business might experience slow progress if you are nonchalant towards utilizing the power of social media marketing.

Right from the beginning, online communities have been an integral part of the Internet, and social media today has been widely accepted all over the world. As a matter fact, are there are estimated to be about 2.62 billion online social media users, and by 2021 it is expected that this value will rise above 3 billion.

Therefore, social media is the best marketing platform for businesses, even more so for business owners that wish to broaden their reach. Finding and applying proven social media techniques is paramount to achieving this goal.

We shall be looking at a few essential social media tools that will give you an edge in effective marketing and business growth.

There Is No Specific Formula for Successful Marketing

According to Puranjay Singh, although a good number of experts have written books and formulas that are believed to be generally effective in marketing, they are sometimes not effective. Creating and publishing posts as often as possible might work for someone else but not for you. This article might sound very affirmative and compelling to follow; nevertheless, there is no specific written formula for successful online marketing.

The uniqueness of every brand or business depends on the problem they are offering a solution to and the nature of the audience involved. Not to mention that social media is ever changing and so is the character of those involved. This makes it even more difficult to have a generalized approach to building a brand online.

Would your approach towards marketing a florist and an eatery online be the same? Of course not. You must first carry out a careful study of your audience, then figure out the best way to reach out and turn them into customers for each business.

To measure your performance as an online marketer, below are a few tools that can be benefic al to you.

Content curation app, DrumUp provides you with content that improves your engagement. This app helps you save time by creating an account for mu tiple account management.

Image optimization app PicMonkey, this enables you to do justice to your images. It also has canvases for different purposes and ready-made templates to suit your needs.

With Google Analytics you can monitor your efforts and know which of your social media platforms are most effective for your online marketing.

Social Mention is a social media monitoring tool that helps you monitor things such as competition, important keywords, and brand mentions.

Engaged Following Is A Prerequisite for High ROI

Every social media marketer focus should be on their ROI, except if you aren't looking forward to making any progress. Building a followership is always a challenge in the initial stages. This is because it takes time and quality content to attract your audience and make them stick around unlike TV and radio station marketing that doesn't require as much effort.

Irrespective of the quality of your content at the beginning, you might still record a low rate of engagement. But applying the right approach and consistently publishing quality content will enable you to achieve that ROI you desire.

Creating A Specific Marketing Strategy Is Important

Research has shown that a large number of marketer's lack strategies to reach their target audience. To build an audience of active followers, creating a marketing strategy is paramount. What is effective content?

- Content that brings about the desired response from an audience

- Content that is relevant to an audience

- Content with an engaging storyline

Challenges Marketers Face with Content Creation

- Inability to monitor the progress of your efforts - to overcome this get a social media monitoring app

- The difficulty in creating content that will captive and engage the targeted audience.

- Limited time to create quality content - this can be dealt with using content curat on apps.

- Difficulty in matching content and required volume.

It is crucial to documert your strategy as it helps you stay focused and confident in your actions.

Publicity Can Come in Different Ways

Just like in the physical world, people promote their businesses and brands through the referral method of "tell someone to tell someone" which could be done by customers, fans, employees or business partners. This can also be applied to social media marketing. Building a good relationship with your online customers will encourage them to promote your brand by introducing your business to their friends and family. Positive feeds and testimonies from your customers are also beneficial.

You can also pay online influencers with a large following to promote your product and services on their platform for a specific period.

You could also partner with other businesses and strike a deal with them. This may require you to promote each other's products and services on your respective platforms. You could also leverage your employees into promoting the business and show your appreciation with incentives.

Ability to Understand the Significance of Data Is Crucial.

Until you can understand the information behind your data and capitalize on it for improvement, limitations will keep locking up your business. This is to say that data interpretation is of great necessity in the process of marketing.

Data itself is limited in action and depends on you for specific clarification. No algorithm can detect the impression people have about your business. Therefore, it is your sole responsibility to have a proper understanding of the data your content generates.

It'll be disastrous for your brand if you build your strategy around data alone. Utilizing the information from your data and applying other formulas to create an effective strategy should be non-negotiable.

As observed, businesses tend to grow faster on social media when there is an interaction between the audience and the marketer. Never neglect your audience if you desire continuous growth.

Focus also on your connection with people outside of social media. Your ability to maintain cordial relationships with your clients should be of the utmost importance.

Strange Social Media Tips That Work

Above, we have covered some proven social media secrets. Now, let us take a look at some strange tips that can help your brand.

Stir Controversy

Marketers who know what they are doing utilize controversy as a means of driving social engagement and traffic. Including the element of controversy in your social media campaigns aids in the following:

- Creating a buzz about your brand or organization

- Pushes massive traffic to your profiles on social media

- Enhances your engagement metrics and follower base

So, how do you develop controversy? Below are a few of the best methods:

Take a different view regarding generally accepted information or facts. For example, if everyone detests a vehicle model, you can gain attention by going the opposite route.

Talk about a taboo subject in your field. For example, if you are into dog training, then speak about using electric collars for dog training.

Pick on Trending Hashtags

As you must be aware, Hashtags aid in classifying or grouping posts on social media. For example, #NewYear.

Additionally, trending hashtags are those trending on a specific day or time. For example: On 25th December each year, #Christmas is a trending hashtag.

This strategy needs you to utilize trending hashtags on your posts to amass peak exposure. But, how do you find a trending hashtags list? There are lots of tools like Trendsmap that can help you out with that. However, in using Hashtags, you need to be careful of the following:

Don't Use Excess Hashtags. Except if an individual has lots of patience, he or she won't go through a lengthy list of hashtags. Place the most significant ones at the start and the most entertaining ones at the end. These are two locations individuals have a high likelihood of reading.

Don't Develop Long Hashtags: Since it is more difficult to read without spaces, restrict them to four words

Don't Utilize Hashtags That Beg for Followers. Having lots of followers is great but having real and engaged individuals is better. Begging for people to follow you is not professional. Stay away from hashtags like #like4like or anything that others would see as pandering.

Don't Forget to Read Through. If you leave spaces out of some words, they will read differently.

Tag an Influencer

An influencer is a personality on social media who has lots of impact on his or her followers. Influencers create relevant content, curate and share the content of others. Aside from that, they are also an excellent source of industry information and news.

Generally, followers act based on the opinions and advice of influencers. They influence their followers' decisions.

But, how exactly can influencers aid you in achieving your social media marketing objectives? It is easy. Say, for example, you wrote a post about freelance writing and tagged a recognized personality on social media. If the influencer you tagged likes your post and retweets or shares it with his followers, your post would instantly be exposed to lots of people.

Make Use of Emojis

Social media is a place filled with lots of businesses trying to grab as many viewers as possible. So, how do you ensure your brand is heard? Why not try emojis?

Emojis tend to capture the eyes of viewers because they are appealing. Additionally, they also make your posts seem more genuine.

Observe Your Competitors

Copying everything your competitor does is not good for business. But checking out other accounts can get your creative juices going.

Find out these facts about your competitors and other leading social media brands. What hashtags are they using? What types of posts are garnering lots of shares or comments?

You can also look at those who have the most interaction with your competitors and follow them. If they are taking time to interact with your competitor, there is a huge possibility that they will also engage with you as well.

Aside from this, you could also try liking or following the posts of your competitors. Just because they are your competitors, it does not mean you can't be friends.

Chapter 12:
Double Down on Social Media Marketing NOW

The benefits of Social Media Marketing cannot be overemphasized. Now is the time to take advantage of this wonderful strategy if you want to grow your business. At present, social media marketing is one of the cheapest means of reaching your customers. It is a re-source that a lot of companies are not taking advantage of yet. But it can have a massive impact on your marketing if you do it correctly.

You need to double down on social media marketing now because it won't always remain as cheap as it is. Over time, the cost is likely going to rise, and it will be more difficult for you as a brand to corner the market as opposed to right now. That is not all. All your clients and potential clients are on social media right now which is why you need to take advantage and reach them soon.

Twitter, Instagram and Facebook are great platforms which will help you go from unknown to widely known. You need to take advantage of these platforms.

Above, I have provided you with many strategies that you can read and implement to make your brand a social media juggernaut. Now, all that is left is for you to invest and use these strategies to draw in loyal subscribers.

If you know you are not taking advantage of social media, then these strategies will certainly be of help. By the time you complete this book, you will have a comprehensive understanding of why social media marketing is important and why you should channel more of your marketing efforts into it.

So why wait? Take that step today and watch yourself become the next social media millionaire.

If you find this book helpful in anyway a review to support my endeavors is much appreciated.

Donald Reammsei

Crushing It with Social Media Marketing

[151]